The Promise of His Appearing

Peter J. Leithart, *The Promise of His Appearing: An Exposition of Second Peter*
© 2004 by Peter J. Leithart

Published by Canon Press, P.O. Box 8741, Moscow, ID 83843
800-488-2034 / www.canonpress.org

13 14 15 16 17 18   9 8 7 6 5 4 3 2

Cover design by Paige Atwood.
Printed in the United States of America.

Unless otherwise noted, all Scripture quotations are from the New American Standard Bible®, Copyright © 1960, 1962, 1963, 1968, 1971, 1972, 1973, 1975, 1977, 1995 by The Lockman Foundation. Used by permission.

Library of Congress Cataloging-in-Publication Data

Leithart, Peter J.
  The promise of His appearing : an exposition of Second Peter / by Peter J.
  Leithart.
      p. cm.
  Includes index.
  ISBN 1-59128-026-5
  1. Bible. N.T. Peter, 2nd—Criticism, interpretation, etc. 2. Bible. N.T. Peter, 2nd—Prophecies. 3. Realized eschatology. I. Title.

BS2795.6.P7L45 2004
227'.9306—dc22
                                    2004022136

The

PROMISE

of His

APPEARING

An Exposition of Second Peter

PETER J. LEITHART

CANON PRESS
Moscow, Idaho

**To read more about the following titles by
Peter J. Leithart, visit www.canonpress.org**

A Son to Me
An Exposition of 1 & 2 Samuel

From Silence to Song
The Davidic Liturgical Revolution

Against Christianity

A House For My Name
A Survey of the Old Testament

Blessed Are the Hungry
Meditations on the Lord's Supper

Heroes of the City of Man
A Christian Guide to Select Ancient Literature

Ascent to Love
A Guide to Dante's Divine Comedy

Brightest Heaven of Invention
A Christian Guide to Six Shakespeare Plays

Wise Words
Family Stories that Bring the Proverbs to Life

CONTENTS

To Smith

May you be among
Those who have insight
Who shine brightly
Like the bright firmament of heaven

ACKNOWLEDGEMENTS

In the course of preparing this brief commentary, I realized that I have spent more time with 2 Peter than with any other New Testament book. Though I have not devoted exclusive attention to it for over fifteen years, I have returned to it again and again. Sometime in the murky *Urzeit* of the late 1980s, I first taught through the book in a Sunday School class at Cherokee Presbyterian Church in Woodstock, Georgia. It was the first book I preached through when I took a pastoral call in 1989 at the Reformed Heritage Presbyterian Church, Birmingham, Alabama, and I taught it again in a Sunday School class at the Cambridge Presbyterian Church, Cambridge, U.K. More recently, I delivered several lectures on the epistle at the 1999 Biblical Horizons Summer Conference, and finally taught the book to a group of friends in Moscow who have gathered for dinner and Bible study for the past several years. Peter's second epistle, in short, is an old friend, and I hope that these various opportunities to teach through the book have given me some measure of familiarity with and insight into its contents. But *judicet lector*.

In addition to the churches that have shown interest in my work on 2 Peter over the years, I wish to thank Doug Jones of

Canon Press, who continues to be far more generous and gentle with me and my books than either of us deserves. Jared Miller too has been an invaluable assistance, noticing incoherencies in my writing and forcing me to clarify, and Lucy Jones has also assisted in moving messy manuscripts to finished books.

Most of my books during the past several years have been dedicated to one of my children. The present volume is due to be dedicated to my sixth and, if present trends continue, my last son, Smith. It is deeply appropriate that this commentary on an "apocalyptic" epistle should be dedicated to Smith, who is no stranger to signs and wonders in the heavens. He was born in Huntington, England, while I was doing my doctoral work at Cambridge, and I'll never forget tearing through the night in our uncertain Freight Rover, with the Hale-Bopp comet guiding us to the hospital. We considered working some reference to Hale-Bopp into his name but finally decided against it. Yet I have amused myself with the thought that the auspicious birth is a portent of greatness, but more importantly I trust that Smith will not be among the stars that fall from the heavens or the elements that melt with intense heat. I trust that he will instead be among those who shine brightly in the expanse of heaven, like a star forever and ever.

1

THE FIRST-CENTURY CONTEXT

This book is not a technical commentary on the Greek text of 2 Peter (though the Greek will be appealed to as necessary or when I want to show off), and it does not give a detailed exposition of every verse of the letter. Instead, it lays out a broad interpretation of the letter, and, more importantly, it lays out a broad interpretive *framework* for it. To do this I will focus on a set of specific issues within the letter, all of which are related in some way to the eschatological teaching of the book, which I argue is central to Peter's intentions. No doubt I have made some errors of interpretation on small and perhaps even larger issues, but I hope that this reading is plausible enough to make some contribution to the scholarship on the epistle and to shift the context for discussion of its contents.

A significant shift in orientation and context is, I believe, necessary to make sense both of 2 Peter and of New Testament eschatology generally. The sort of shift I hope for can be easily stated: I offer a preterist reading of 2 Peter and hope that this book will contribute to making the preterist framework of interpretation a more reputable player in New Testament studies. *Preterism* is the view that prophecies about an imminent "day of judgment" scattered throughout the New Testament were fulfilled in the apostolic age by the destruction of Jerusalem in A.D. 70, the event that brought a final end to the structures and orders of the Old Creation or Old Covenant. Within this framework, Peter is dealing with issues facing the churches of the first century as the day approaches when the old world will be destroyed. Jesus said, "Truly I say to you, there are some of those who are standing here who shall not taste death until they see the Son of Man coming in His kingdom" (Mt. 16:28), and I argue that Peter wrote his second letter to remind the readers of that specific prophecy of Jesus and to encourage them to cling to that promise of His appearing.

For the purposes of this book, preterism is not merely a way of interpreting New Testament prophecy but also provides a framework for understanding New Testament theology as a whole. In part, this is nothing more than an effort to understand the New Testament in its historical context. The issues and debates that dominated the New Testament era were largely about the relation of Jews and Gentiles, and derived directly from the gospel's announcement of a new people of God, within which circumcision and uncircumcision are equally meaningless. Preterist interpretation means trying to understand the New Testament in the light of this struggle without retrojecting post-Reformation debates into the text.[1] Further, an important goal of preterist interpretation is to reckon with the influence that the threat and promise of Jesus' imminent coming, which affects nearly every book of the New Testament, had on the shape of New Testament theology. For example, a preterist framework generates such questions as "Is it possible that the typology of the church in the wilderness (in Hebrews, for instance) had specific reference to the first-century situation?" and "What is unique about the organization, worship, and life of the church in the period between A.D. 30–70?" and "What unique role

---

[1] This does not mean that the New Testament has nothing to say about post-Reformation debates, only that those debates were not the same as the debates of the New Testament era itself.

did the first-century church play in redemptive history, and how is this related to the fall of Jerusalem?"

Though preterist interpretations have been around for several centuries,[2] only in the past several decades has this view been endorsed by Protestant interpreters. A number of conservative Reformed commentators, notably J. Marcellus Kik, Kenneth Gentry, David Chilton, Gary DeMar, R. C. Sproul, and James Jordan, have defended some variety of preterism, and in mainstream New Testament studies a preterist interpretation of Jesus' "little apocalypse" (Mt. 24; Mk. 13; Lk. 21) has been promoted by G. B. Caird, N. T. Wright, Marcus Borg, and others.[3] These commentators all agree that Jesus describes the end of the Old Covenant order or Judaism by using language of cosmic collapse, and several argue that John does the same in Revelation.

The prophecies of 2 Peter 3 have also been interpreted as foretelling the final collapse of the Old Creation in A.D. 70. For example, centuries ago John Owen linked the language of 2 Peter 3:8–13 with the prophecy of Isaiah 65 to argue that Peter was not predicting the end of the physical universe but the end of the Old Covenant order.[4] David Chilton followed Owen in this conclusion,[5] and more recently John Noe and others have presented similar

---

[2] See Arthur Wainwright, *Mysterious Apocalypse: Interpreting the Book of Revelation* (Eugene, Ore.: Wipf & Stock, 2001), 63–64, for a brief discussion of the preterist interpretation of Revelation.

[3] Gentry, *Before Jerusalem Fell: Dating the Book of Revelation* (Tyler: ICE, 1989); Chilton, *Days of Vengeance: An Exposition of the Book of Revelation* (Tyler: Dominion Press, 1987); Jordan, *A Brief Reader's Guide To Revelation* (Niceville: Transfiguration Press, 1999); Caird, *Language and Imagery of the Bible* (Grand Rapids: Eerdmans, 1980); Wright, *Jesus and the Victory of God* (London: SPCK, 1996); Borg, *Conflict, Holiness and Politics in the Teachings of Jesus* (Harrisburg: Trinity Press International, [1984] 1998).

[4] John Owen, *The Works of John Owen*, 16 vols. (London: Banner of Truth, 1965–68), 9:134–135.

[5] Chilton, *Days of Vengeance*, 540–545.

arguments.[6] Mainstream evangelical and liberal commentators on
2 Peter, however, continue to be almost completely unaware of
preterism as an interpretive option.[7]

In a sense, mainstream scholarship's failure to consider preterist
treatments of 2 Peter is the understandable result of the weaknesses
of the preterist readings of the book that have generally been offered. David Chilton's treatment, for example, focuses exclusively on 2 Peter 3, since that is the chapter which is most overtly
eschatological. To be fair, it should be said that Chilton's discussion
takes place in the context of a commentary on Revelation 21:1, so
he can hardly be expected to treat the entire book of 2 Peter. Yet, this
same narrow attention to chapter 3 is characteristic of preterist
treatments I have seen elsewhere. The important question of
whether 2 Peter 3 predicts an event that took place in the first century has overshadowed the equally important questions of how
chapter 3 fits with the rest of Peter's letter and whether the whole
of the letter might be understood preteristically.

---

[6] Noe, *Beyond the End Times* (Bradford, Penn.: Preterist Resources, 1999). A number of web sites also offer preterist readings of NT prophecy: preterist.org,
planetpreterist.com, preteristhomepage.com, and preteristarchive.com. The content of these sites is very diverse. Alongside much insightful material, many articles
endorse a heretical version of preterism that denies the future return of Christ.

[7] In his solidly evangelical commentary, Douglas Moo (*2 Peter, Jude* [NIV Applica-
tion Commentary; Grand Rapids: Zondervan, 1996]) occasionally refers to passages that use the imagery of cosmic collapse to describe historical events, but this
plays virtually no role in his discussion of the letter as a whole. Late in the book,
Moo acknowledges that "many early Christians looked eagerly for Christ to return
and take them to glory" and that "Peter himself encouraged believers to recognize
that 'the end of all things is near' (1 Peter 4:7)" but fails to consider seriously the
possibility that Peter was writing about an imminent event. The same goes for
Norman Hillyer, *1 and 2 Peter, Jude* (New International Biblical Commentary; New
Testament Series no. 16; Peabody, Mass.: Hendrickson, 1992), and Michael Green,
2 Peter and Jude (Tyndale New Testament Commentaries; rev. ed.; Leicester:
InterVarsity, 1987). Richard Bauckham raises the possibility of something like a
preterist interpretation at a number of points but rejects it (*Jude, 2 Peter,* Word Biblical Commentary no. 50 [Waco, Tex.: Word, 1983]).

Another difficulty with Chilton's treatment is that he is content to point to passages where the destruction of the "heavens and earth" is obviously used to describe an historical event, the collapse of a political-religious order. It is increasingly acknowledged among New Testament scholars that this language can be used in this metaphorical sense, but it also has to be established that Peter is using this terminology in this way. The language of resurrection, to take a parallel example, can be used to describe Israel's national resurrection (e.g., Ezek. 37), but the church has never taken the resurrection of 1 Corinthians 15 in this sense. I cannot say that this commentary moves from possibility to absolute certainty, but I hope to show that within 2 Peter the probability that Peter is using the terminology metaphorically is quite high.

Finally, I should note that many of the preterist interpretations of Peter's letter have been offered by commentators who believe that *all* New Testament prophecies were fulfilled in A.D. 70, even the resurrection of the dead that Paul predicts in 1 Corinthians 15.[8] This book will not address this viewpoint in any detail, but I must register here my strongest disagreement with it, since I consider it heretical. Though commentators sometimes twist 1 Corinthians 15 into a prophecy of the national resurrection of Israel or a description of bodiless life after death, it is perfectly evident in the context that this is not what Paul is talking about. To come to the latter conclusion, one must thoroughly overturn the common biblical understanding of "resurrection," turning it into what N. T. Wright has recently called "a new and exciting way of speaking about death."[9] But the structural premise of Paul's entire argument is the parallel between Jesus' resurrection and ours, and Jesus was at pains to show His disciples that He rose from the dead with a

---

[8] See, for example, Max King, *The Cross and the Parousia of Christ: The Two Dimensions of One Age-Changing Eschaton* (Warren: Parkman Road Church of Christ, 1987).

[9] *The Resurrection of the Son of God* (Minneapolis: Fortress, 2003).

body that could consume food, that had bones, that could be touched and felt (e.g., Lk. 24:39). Resurrection, to cite Wright again, is not "life after death" but "life after life after death."[10]

Nor can 1 Corinthians 15 be a description of the national resurrection of Israel, the formation of a "New Israel" during the first century. While such a resurrection of Israel did occur in the first century, Paul is not talking about that in 1 Corinthians 15. The resurrection that Paul describes will occur at the "end," when all rule and authority has been subjected to the reign of Jesus and when the "last enemy," death, has been defeated (vv. 24–26). Again, if language means anything at all, this cannot be a description of something that happened in the first century, for it is too obvious to mention that death has not been defeated. Paul is not talking about what John calls the "first resurrection" (Rev. 20:5), whatever that might be, but about the resurrection that takes place after the Millennium, the resurrection to judgment, the resurrection followed by the final evacuation of death and Hades (Rev. 20:11–15).

Further, the "hyper-preterist" must reduce the Millennium of Revelation 20 to a symbolic description of a forty-year period between the resurrection of Jesus and the destruction of Jerusalem. Whatever the difficulties of Revelation 20, one clear conclusion is that the "thousand years" symbolizes a significant period of time. When not used literally, the number one thousand is used consistently to describe things that are literally far more than one thousand:

> For every beast of the forest is Mine, the cattle on a thousand hills. (Ps. 50:10)

> For a thousand years in Thy sight are like yesterday when it passes by or as a watch in the night. (Ps. 90:4)

---

[10] Ibid., 201.

He remembered His covenant forever, the word which He commanded to a thousand generations. (Ps. 105:8)

It is nonsense to use "one thousand years" to symbolize a generation.

By arguing that the entire letter is about Jesus' prophecy concerning the coming crisis of Jerusalem and Judaism, therefore, I hope to bolster the preterist interpretation of chapter 3 and make the preterist framework more plausible to students of 2 Peter. To gain a hearing, however, I aim for much more than a hearing, for I will argue that the argument of the letter is only coherent if it is interpreted in a preterist framework. Along the way, therefore, I highlight five reasons (bold-faced, indented, and labeled as "Knock-Down Arguments" for the reader's convenience) why the letter *must* be interpreted preteristically if it is going to be accepted as a genuine letter at all. By the end of the book, I expect the opposing views to be lying on the canvas in a state of semiconsciousness. But the best argument for a preterist interpretation of 2 Peter will be the sense it is able to make of the letter as a whole. Persuasion, if it comes, will come more through abduction than deduction.

WHO WROTE 2 PETER TO WHOM?

Questions of authorship, date, and original audience can seem like the tedious preoccupations of theological nerds. There is a good reason for that perception: these discussions are often tedious when they are not far worse. Yet several introductory questions are relevant to my interpretation of 2 Peter and require some attention. This section might be labeled "Please Bear with the Nerd."

Even in the early church, the letter's authenticity was questioned. Although Origen referred to it without hesitation, Eusebius mentioned that Peter left one "disputed" epistle. Nowadays it is common, even among evangelical commentators, to see the letter as an example of *pseudepigrapha*—a work written under the name of an authoritative figure by someone else. Scholars deny

Peter's authorship for various reasons. Some understand the personal allusions contained in the book as a literary device common in ancient pseudepigraphic writings. The self-identification of the author as "Sim[e]on Peter" rather than "Peter" (cf. 1 Pet. 1:1), it is argued, is an obvious attempt by the author to link himself with the Simon Peter of gospels. The claim to be an eyewitness on the Mount of Transfiguration (1:16–18) is another of the author's clumsy attempts to cloak himself in Peter's mantle, but to the discerning modern scholar the phrase "holy mountain" (1:18) gives him away as a second-century Christian who was interested in shrines and holy spaces in a way that the real Peter could not have been. The author gives himself away again in 3:16 by referring to "all" of Paul's letters as a fixed collection, which reveals again that he is living much later than the middle of the first century. And he blunders royally in 3:4, when he describes the first generation of Christians as "fathers" who have "fallen asleep," for how can he be Peter if the apostolic generation is dead? Some have argued, furthermore, that the situation described by the epistle is too late for Peter's day (Peter died c. 65), since the heresies described in 2 Peter 2 are like second-century gnosticism, and it is of course impossible that there could be any first-century movements like them. Other scholars have pointed to the marked difference in style between 1 Peter and 2 Peter, pointing out (rightly) that the Greek style of the latter is far more stilted and ornamented than that of the former, and recognizing that it is improbable that a single writer could write, say, *both* children's tales about adventures in a world called Narnia *and* erudite historical studies of English literature. In content, finally, the book employs a number of Hellenistic terms and concepts that would have been over the head of a Galilean fisherman.

I will not take time to defend Petrine authorship in any thorough way, though I trust the reader has caught the drift of my views from the sarcastic tone of the preceding paragraph. Still, several points need to be addressed more directly. Clearly, a preterist reading of 2 Peter—one that claims that the letter is concerned with the end of the Old Creation in A.D. 70—has an investment in the authorship question. If, as is commonly believed, Peter died under Nero in the mid-60s and if Peter wrote the letter, then the letter must have been written before the fall of Jerusalem. Assuming that Peter died before A.D. 70, there are a number of logical possibilities: (A) Peter wrote the letter prior to A.D. 70; (B) Someone wrote the letter under Peter's name prior to A.D. 70; (C) Someone wrote the letter under Peter's name after A.D. 70.

Options A and B could support a preterist interpretation (though neither requires a preterist interpretation), but option C implies either that the letter is not about A.D. 70 or, if it is about A.D. 70, it is not a prophecy (since it was written after the fact). Most contemporary scholars prefer Option C, but there is one decisive reason why this must be rejected, and this same reason establishes Option A as the only possibility (assuming that the writer is the least bit honest). In 1:16, Peter assures his readers that the prophecies he reminds them about are reliable, since he was an eyewitness of the majesty of Christ on the "holy mountain" of the Transfiguration. The problem here is not simply a moral one—i.e., the fact that if the writer is not Peter, he is lying about being an eyewitness to the Transfiguration. Commentators normally dodge this objection by saying that all the readers would have recognized the pseudepigraphic nature of the letter and would have "played along." The author's claim to have been with Jesus on the mountain would have been no more a lie than Lew Wallace's claim that Ben Hur witnessed the crucifixion. Fiction is not subject to the same standards of truth and falsity as a historical record.[11] We suspend disbelief and play along.

<hr/>

[11] Bauckham, who claims that 2 Peter is pseudepigraphal, says of 1:16: "it is . . . beside the point to connect the emphasis on eyewitness testimony with the

The idea that pseudepigraphic writings were common and commonly accepted in the early church is in fact untrue. Church fathers frequently condemned pseudepigrapha as forgeries and without any authority. The more serious problem, however, is internal to 2 Peter: the argument of chapter 1 simply collapses if Peter is not Peter. Peter cites his presence at the Transfiguration to prove that "the prophetic word" can be relied on. If Peter was already dead and someone else was writing under his name, the writer's opponents have an obvious response: "No, you weren't!" The mockers who are denying the "promise of His coming" (1:16; 3:4) would not be impressed with a claim that the promise of Jesus' coming was backed up by an eyewitness who was not really an eyewitness.[12] I'm with the fathers: if the writer was not Peter, then he was an unscrupulous liar who is not worthy of our confidence in any other respect.

Neither Option B nor C can handle Peter's affirmation in 1:16. If the letter has a persuasive and coherent argument at all, then it must have been written by Peter, and if Peter wrote the letter, then it must have been written before the fall of Jerusalem.

But to whom?

---

pseudepigraphical nature of the letter. The author is not trying to bolster his own authority by claiming, falsely, to be an eyewitness of the Transfiguration. He is simply adducing Peter's testimony as evidence that the event took place as he narrates it, and puts it in the first person form because of the literary convention he is following. In another sort of literary work he could have reported Peter's testimony in the third person, to the same effect" (*Jude, 2 Peter*, 216). To the first point: Bauckham notwithstanding, it is surely the case that the writer is bolstering his own authority by claiming to be an eyewitness. Anyone who says of an event "I saw it happen" is attempting to support his competence to report on the incident. To the second point: third-person testimony does *not* have the same effect as eyewitness testimony, as even the least competent lawyer could have told Bauckham.

[12] This point is all the stronger when we recall the significance of witnesses in biblical law and Israelite social life. The Ten Words condemn a witness who gives false testimony, and false witnesses were severely punished (Deut. 5, 19).

ALIENS OF THE DIASPORA

The recipients of 2 Peter are not named in the book, but there are several hints and clues that help to identify them, at least in general terms. In 2 Peter 3:1, Peter says, "This is now, beloved, the second letter I am writing to you in which I am stirring up your sincere mind by way of reminder." Possibly Peter means a letter no longer extant, but it is more likely that he is referring to the letter that we have in our Bibles as 1 Peter. The strongest evidence for this comes from a comparison of the phrasing and themes of the two letters. John H. Elliott's summary is worth citing:[13]

1 Peter	*2 Peter*
1:1 "Peter"	1:1 "Peter"; cf. 3:1
1:1 etc. "elect"	1:10, "election"; cf. Jude 2
1:2 greeting	1:2; cf. Jude 2
1:3, 17 "Father"	1:17
1:7, 13; 4:13; 5:1, 4	1:16, revelation, coming of
1:7 etc. "glory"	1:3 etc.
1:10–11 "prophets"	1:20–21; 3:2
1:14–16, etc. "holy"	3:11, 14; Jude 20
1:15, 19 [spotless]	3:14
1:17; 4:5, 17 "judgment"	3:7
1:19 [spotless]	3:14; cf. 2:13
1:22; 2:17; 3:8; 4:8; 5:9 [love]	3:7
2:12; 3:2 *epoptueo*	1:16
2:16 [freedom]	2:19
3:19 "disobedient angel-spirits"	2:4; cf. Jude 6
3:20, Noah, Flood	2:5; 3:6
4:2–4 [dissipation of unbelievers]	2:5; 3:6

[13] *1 Peter,* Anchor Bible, vol. 37B (New York: Doubleday, 2000), 141. Elliott does not accept Petrine authorship of 2 Peter and cites these parallels merely to establish "affinities" between the two books, suggesting that "both documents are products of different authors of a Petrine circle in Rome" (141). See the similar list of parallels in Hillyer, *1 and 2 Peter, Jude,* 15.

4:7 [end of all things]	3:10
4:11d [doxology]	3:18b
4:19 "creator"	3:5

The fact that both letters deal with Jesus' coming is of particular importance for my purposes. Peter says specifically that he had earlier taught his readers about "the power and coming of our Lord Jesus Christ" (2 Pet. 1:16), and in chapter 3 he reminds them of teaching them about events of the "last days" and the promise of a "new heavens and new earth" (3:3, 13). In both cases, Peter says that he was simply reminding readers of what he had already told them, in the first letter at least and perhaps also in other ways (3:1). The "last days" and the coming "day" of judgment are themes of 1 Peter. As Elliott's list indicates, a coming judgment or revelation is mentioned several times in 1 Peter:

> [You are] protected by the power of God through faith for a salvation ready to be revealed in the last time. (1:5)

> In this [affliction] you greatly rejoice, even though now for a little while, if necessary, you have been distressed by various temptations, that the proof of your faith, being more precious than gold which is perishable, even though tested by fire, may be found to result in praise and glory and honor at the revelation of Jesus Christ. (1:6–7)

> Gird the loins of your mind for action, keep sober in spirit, fix your hope completely on the grace to be brought to you at the revelation of Jesus Christ. (1:13)

> [The Gentiles] are surprised that you do not run with them into the same excess of dissipation, and they malign you; but they shall give account to Him who is ready to judge the living and the dead. . . . The end of all things is at hand. (4:4–5, 7)

Beloved, do not be surprised at the fiery ordeal among you, which comes upon you for your testing, as though some strange thing were happening to you; but to the degree that you share the sufferings of Christ, keep on rejoicing; so that also at the revelation of His glory, you may rejoice with exultation. (4:13)

For it is time for judgment to begin with the household of God; and if it begins with us first, what will be the outcome for those who do not obey the gospel of God? (4:17)

Therefore, I exhort the elders among you, as your fellow elder and witness of the sufferings of Christ, and a partaker also of the glory that is to be revealed, shepherd the flock of God among you. . . . And when the Chief Shepherd appears, you will receive the unfading wreath of glory. (5:1, 4)

In several of these passages, Peter explicitly states that there is an event on his readers' immediate horizon (1 Pet. 1:5; 4:4–5, 7, 17). Even some of the passages that lack an explicit time reference refer to an event that is about to happen. The "revelation of Jesus Christ" in 1 Peter 1:7 and 1:13 is doubtless the same event as the coming of "a salvation . . . to be revealed in the last time" in 1:5, and therefore the time reference of 1:5 ("ready to be revealed") applies also to the manifestation of Jesus in verses 7 and 13. The revelation of Jesus, moreover, is likely the same event as the appearance of the Chief Shepherd (1 Pet. 5:4). Given these passages, it makes sense for Peter to say that he has already "made known to you the power and coming of our Lord Jesus Christ" (2 Pet. 1:16) and that his "second letter" is written to remind his readers of "words spoken beforehand . . . by your apostles" (2 Pet. 3:1), including Peter himself.

The connection between 1 and 2 Peter makes a prima facie case for a preterist interpretation of the latter. If 1 Peter is about a revelation that is "ready" to come, about an "end of all things" that is "at hand," about a judgment that is "ready to begin" at the house of God, then 2 Peter, which is a reminder of things taught in the previous letter, must be about the same topic. Anyone reading the second letter with a knowledge of the first (which Peter assumes) would naturally assume that he was talking about the *same* imminent "coming" that he talked about in the earlier letter.

Knock-Down Argument #1:

Peter wrote his second letter on the theme of the coming of Jesus, which he says was also a theme of his first letter, which is 1 Peter. Since 1 Peter's teaching about the "coming" of Jesus highlights its imminence, 2 Peter must be dealing with the same looming event.

If Peter wrote both letters to the same Christians, who *are* these recipients? 1 Peter 1:1–2 describes them as "those who reside as aliens, scattered" throughout Asia Minor. "Aliens" is a literal description of their geographic and political condition, rather than a description of a spiritual condition. They are residing in an alien land rather than in their homeland. Peter also describes them as being "scattered," employing a Greek word related to *diaspora*. By Peter's time, *diaspora* had become a technical term for the dispersion of the Jews from the time of the Babylonian captivity, and so it is possible that Peter is writing to the scattered Jews, living as aliens outside the land of promise. If so, these are Jewish *believers*, not Jews in general. They are a chosen people, as Israel was, but they are chosen to "obey Jesus Christ and be sprinkled with His blood," and they are awaiting the revelation of Jesus Christ (1 Pet. 1:7). Peter may be writing, then, to diaspora Jews who converted to Christ through the preaching of various apostles, perhaps including Paul (1 Pet. 1:1; 2 Pet. 3:15).

That the recipients are Jewish believers may be supported by Peter's use of Old Testament terms and phrases to describe them and their relationship with Jesus. Jesus Christ is the cornerstone laid "in Zion" (1 Pet. 2:6). Those who are outside the community are "Gentiles" (1 Pet. 2:12; 4:3), and therefore the recipients are to think of themselves as "Jews." Even the description "not being a people" (1 Pet. 2:10) is drawn from Hosea's description of the adultery and restoration of Israel. According to Hosea, Yahweh treated them as "not a people" but then wooed them back to become His people (Hos. 1:10; 2:23).[14] Yet commentators on 1 Peter almost all agree that the letter was written to *Gentiles* and give several arguments to support this conclusion. One is that Peter describes his readers as formerly being controlled by lust and ignorance, committed to a "futile way of life inherited from your forefathers" (1 Pet. 1:14, 18). These seem to describe people who have formerly been worshipers of "vain" or "futile" idols. Further, 4:3–4 recall that the readers have engaged in "abominable idolatries."[15]

I do not find these arguments for a Gentile audience persuasive. Peter recognized that the Jews were "ignorant" in regard to Christ (Acts 3:17), and even Peter's description of the "futile way of life" inherited from their forefathers and their "idolatries" might reasonably be applied to Jews. For many centuries, after all, Israel had been a nation of idolaters, setting up high places, worshiping Baals and Asherah, burning incense to golden calves. Paul certainly was capable of describing Israel's history as a history of futility and idolatry. In Romans 1, he brings God's case against humanity in general, but his indictment includes a sharp attack on Jews in particular. When Paul says that foolish men have "exchanged the glory

---

[14] The famed early church historian Eusebius understood 1 Peter as a letter addressed to the Jews of the dispersion.

[15] Hillyer's summary is concise: "The readers Peter had in mind seem to have been a mixed group, though mainly Gentile Christians, for he refers to their pre-conversion days in terms of ignorance of the true God (1:14), their earlier way of life (1:18), previous spiritual darkness (2:18), and pagan vices (4:3–4)" (*1 and 2 Peter, Jude*, 4).

of the incorruptible God for an image in the form of corruptible man and of birds and four-footed animals and crawling creatures" (Rom. 1:23), he is quoting from Psalm 106, which is a poetic description of the golden calf incident. Israel, as much as the Gentiles (or more), had "exchanged the truth of God for a lie, and worshiped and served the creature rather than the Creator" (Rom. 1:25).[16] Jews as much as Gentiles became "futile in their speculations" (Rom. 1:21), and the word "futile" here is the verb form of the noun used in 1 Peter 1:18 (*mataios, mataioo*). More generally, it is not at all unusual for Scripture to describe the Israelites' idolatry as leading to futility,[17] even futility inherited from the fathers:

> Thus says Yahweh, "What injustice did your fathers find in Me, that they went far from Me and walked after emptiness (LXX: *mataios*) and became empty (LXX: *mataioo*)?" (Jer. 2:5)

> Thus says Yahweh, "Do not learn the ways of the nations . . . for the customs of the peoples are futility (LXX: *mataios*); because it is wood cut from the forest, the work of the hands of a craftsman with a cutting tool." (Jer. 10:2–3)

> Every man is stupid, devoid of knowledge; every goldsmith is put to shame by his idols; for his molten images are deceitful, and there is no breath in them. They are worthless (LXX: *mataios*), a work of mockery; in the time of their punishment they will perish. (Jer. 10:14–15)

These references from Jeremiah are particularly important: Jeremiah was warning Judah and Jerusalem of an impending catastrophe because of their devotion to futility; Peter, an apostolic Jeremiah as well as an apostolic Moses (see below), does the same.

[16]Thanks to Kevin Bywater for this suggestion.
[17]Thanks again to Kevin Bywater, who suggested these connections in a phone conversation, May 19, 2003.

The Jewish forefathers' way of life was "futile" in several ways. In Romans, Paul charges that they inherited futile idolatry and human traditions, following in the ways of their fathers, just as many of the kings of Judah and Israel walked in the ways of idolatrous predecessors. Furthermore, the Old Covenant itself did not achieve the end of final salvation and thus was ultimately futile. The law, weak through the flesh, could not bring the forgiveness of sins or the new life of the resurrection (Rom. 8:1–4). While describing the readers as participating in Gentile lusts and idolatries, 1 Peter 4:3–4 clearly distinguishes between the readers and the "Gentiles." With these considerations in mind, I conclude that 1 Peter was addressed to Jewish believers who have been redeemed from Judaism by Christ.[18]

By focusing on Peter's use of *diaspora*, we can be more specific about the circumstances of the original readers. Though this term was used in Jewish literature to describe the scattering of Jews following the Exile, the New Testament uses the word predominantly for another "scattering." After Stephen was stoned, Jews led by Saul began persecuting the church in earnest, and because of this, believers in Jerusalem were "scattered." (In Acts 8:1 the word is the verbal form of *diaspora*, and 8:4 repeats the statement.) Acts 11:19 mentions others scattered by this persecution going out as far as Cyprus, Antioch, and Phoenicia, as if picking up on the story line of 8:1: "So then those who were scattered because of the persecution that arose in connection with Stephen made their way to Phoenicia and Cyprus and Antioch, speaking the word to no one except Jews alone." In the very next verse, we read of the first efforts to proclaim Jesus to Gentiles (11:20). Thus, the diaspora from Jerusalem led immediately to the Gentile mission, which emanated from

---

[18] My preterist interpretation of 2 Peter does not, however, depend on this identification of the audience. Gentile believers scattered through Asia Minor would also have had interest in the impending destruction of the Old Covenant order.

Antioch.[19] The New Testament records a diaspora of the Jerusalem church, scattered because of the attack of another "Babylon" (1 Pet. 5:13), which is Jerusalem. Like other descriptions of Israel (the people, seed of Abraham, sons of God, etc.), the New Testament applies *disapora* predominantly to the church.

This gives us an insight into the situation into which Peter wrote his second letter: the recipients are Jewish believers who are no longer living in Jerusalem, their home city, because of persecution. In 1 Peter, the apostle gives them hope and comfort in the midst of their sufferings, assuring them that a judgment is awaiting their persecutors, which will soon be carried out (1 Pet. 4:3–5, 7, 17; 5:4). Their suffering will be vindicated, the blood of the martyrs will be poured out upon the city, and the Avenger of blood will arise to take vengeance. In this context, 2 Peter 3:1–2 also makes sense—given the passage of time, it is important for Peter to write again to give reassurances. In his first letter, he had used strong language to convey the imminence of the judgment: the "end of all things" is near (1 Pet. 4:7), and it is "time for judgment to begin from the household of God" (4:17). But time passed and more and more of the apostles died, and nothing happened. Some, particularly the persecutors whom the church hoped would be judged, began to mock the Christians' expectation and hope for vindication. They raise doubts that the judgment is going to happen at all, and some believers have broken under the pressure. An apostasy is beginning, and the focus is on the failure of Christ to return. Peter writes to assure his readers that what he predicted in his earlier letter *will* come to pass.

---

[19] I take James 1:1 in the same sense: the "twelve tribes who are dispersed abroad" are Jewish believers who have been scattered by the persecution of Jews. In my view, the only New Testament passage that uses *diaspora* in the typical Jewish sense is John 7:35: "He is not intending to go to the Dispersion among the Greeks, and teach the Greeks, is He?"

Though this reconstruction is admittedly too speculative to use as a basis for a preterist interpretation of 2 Peter, it is obviously consistent with such an interpretation.[20]

STRUCTURE

2 Peter is laid out in roughly a chiastic outline, a fact that will guide us at a number of points in our interpretation of the letter:

A. Fruitfulness in knowledge of Christ, 1:1–11
   B. Reminder of the power and coming of Christ, 1:12–21
      C. False prophets, 2:1–3
         D. God knows how to protect the righteous, 2:4–10a
      C'. False teachers, 2:10b–22
   B'. Reminder of the day of the Lord, 3:1–13
A'. Encouragement to perseverance, 3:14–18

[20] It also fits with portions of Revelation that highlight the unique role that Jewish believers, and their martyrdom, play in the coming of the New Creation. See Revelation 6:9–10; 7:1–8; 14:1–5, 14–20; 16–17. James Jordan's treatment of this theme in Revelation is highly compressed but gets matters exactly right (see *A Brief Readers' Guide to Revelation*, passim).

In the light of all this, the phrase "second letter" is significant. The Greek is "*deuteran ... epistolen*," which echoes with "Deuteronomy" (*deuteros nomos*)—the second giving of the law, and suggests that Peter sees himself in the situation of Moses in Deuteronomy. In Deuteronomy, Moses preached on the law and oversaw a "second giving" of the law for the generation that had grown up in the wilderness to prepare them to enter the land and conquer. The parallels with 2 Peter are numerous. Peter was writing to people who had not seen the "signs and wonders" that Jesus did while on earth. They were not on the "holy mountain," the new Sinai (Exod. 19:23). They did not see the glory of the Lord revealed on the Mountain of Transfiguration. They did not hear the voice on the mountain, but Peter-Moses did, and he comes as a witness to tell them of things which they did not see or hear. Like Deuteronomy, 2 Peter is Peter's "last will and testament" (1:13–14). Because Peter knows that his earthly tabernacle is fading away, he sets down on paper what he has to tell the people, so that when he is gone they will be able to bring things to mind (v. 15). Similarly, Deuteronomy records sermons that Moses delivered at the end of his life. Just as Moses did not enter the Promised Land, Peter will not live to

In a chiasm, the corresponding sections (for example, A and A')
share themes, content, or wording. Within 2 Peter, there are cor-
respondences between the sections in at least the following ways.

A/A': The two A sections are connected by verbal links ("be diligent," 1:10, 15; 3:14) and more generally by the fact that both are
exhortations. They are also linked by the theme of "knowledge"
(1:2, 3, 6, 8; 3:18) and by the fact that both contain blessings (in the
greeting of 1:2 and in the farewell of 3:17–18).

B/B': These sections include language of remembrance and rec-
ollection (1:12, 13, 15; 3:1, 2). Both, moreover, employ the phrase
"know this first of all" (1:20; 3:3), and both are concerned with the
"day" (1:19; 3:12) and the "coming" of Jesus (1:16; 3:4). Substan-
tively, both sections address doubts about the reliability of Jesus'
promise to come to rescue His people.

C/C': These sections are linked by a common concern for false
prophecy or false teaching. Chapter 2 begins with a reference to
Israel's history of false prophecy (v. 1), and one of these false prophets, Balaam, is mentioned in verses 15–16. In both, Peter accuses
his opponents of "sensuality" (2:3, 18), apostasy (2:1, 20–22), and
false words or heresies (2:1, 18). Both sections employ the image of
a "way" or "path" to describe a manner of living (2:2, 15), and both
deal with the greed of the opponents (2:3, 14–15).

D: The central section of Peter's epistle contains his assurance,
based on several Old Testament events, that the Lord will judge

---

see the "new heavens and new earth in which righteousness dwells" (2 Pet. 3:13).
Peter wants to ensure that there is continuity from one generation to the next,
which is certainly a key theme of Deuteronomy as well. As the apostolic generation
(the generation that came out from "Egypt") dies out, he wants to encourage those
who remain to take their inheritance. This setting makes an emphasis on approaching judgment enormously interesting to his audience. They have been scattered
from Jerusalem, the blood of their brothers has been drunk by the harlot, and now
Peter is saying that judgment is going to fall on Jerusalem, that she will not escape
scot-free. Jerusalem is a new Jericho, as it is in Acts and Revelation, ready to fall at
the coming of Peter's "God and Savior," Jesus.

and will rescue His own in the midst of judgment. The beginning of this section is fairly clear: verse 4 turns from a warning about the false prophets to an assurance that the Lord will judge. But the end of the section is more difficult to determine. Verse 9 is the conclusion to the series of "if" statements (vv. 4, 6, 7), but whether the first half of verse 10 concludes this section or begins another is difficult to determine. I have, based on grammatical considerations that we need not detail, divided verse 10 in the middle, following the NASB in seeing verse 10a as the concluding clause of verse 9 and verse 10b as the beginning of a new section of polemic against the false teachers.

One implication of this structure is that the letter is a connected whole, dealing with one main theme, namely, the power and coming of Jesus and false prophets who deny His power and coming. The issue of the "last days" or the "new heavens and new earth" does not arise for the first time at the end of the letter. Given the chiastic connection between the beginning and end, if the timing of "day" at the beginning can be determined with some certainty, so might the other. If I can show that 1:12–21 is about an imminent day of judgment, it will follow that 3:1–13 is as well.

According to John Breck, chiasms not only function "statically" with balancing sections on either side of a central section, but also function "dynamically," so that the text circles in toward a central point. The first of each pair of corresponding sections makes a statement, which the second of the pair amplifies; the writer says *A* and then, what's more, *A'*.[21] With regard to 2 Peter, the structure works as follows.

A / A': Peter urges his readers to put on Christian virtue (A), and, what's more, warns them before of the challenges they will face in living holy lives (A').

[21] Breck, *The Shape of Biblical Language* (Crestwood: St. Vladimir's Seminary Press, 1994).

B/B': Peter can testify to the truth of Jesus' promised coming (B), and, what's more, this promise will be fulfilled in spite of delays and mockery (B').

C/C': The mockers are not worth listening to because they have denied Jesus (C), and, what's more, they will themselves be destroyed (C').

D: We know that God can and will destroy the false teachers and mockers, and rescue His children, because He consistently has done this in the past.

In short, the central thrust of the book as a whole is not merely to give information about the coming day of God. Peter's main goal is pastoral, to prepare the flock for the difficulties ahead and to assure them that God, the Judge of all the earth, will do right and will not let the righteous perish with the wicked when He comes to destroy a new Sodom.

2
A LETTER OF REMINDER

Peter introduces himself at the outset as "Simon" or "Simeon" Peter
(most manuscripts record the latter name), and it is striking that
Peter chooses to introduce himself in this manner (cf. 1 Pet. 1:1).
"Simon" is a Greek translation of Peter's given name, but "Simeon"
is a transliteration closer to the original Hebrew spelling. This
form of Peter's name is used only one other time in the New Testament, in James' summary statement at the Council of Jerusalem:
"Simeon related how God first concerned himself about taking
from among the Gentiles a people for His name" (Acts 15:14). By
introducing himself in this manner, Peter may be giving a clue that
the concerns of the epistle were of particular import to the Jewish
Christians to whom he is writing or that he is dealing with
Judaizing issues raised at the Council. In both Acts 15:14 and 2 Peter 1:1, the Hebraic form of the name is linked with an allusion to
the Gentile world, for "Peter" is a name of Greek origin and
Simeon's report in Acts 15 is about the extension of God's favor to
Gentiles.[1] Right from the outset, Peter identifies himself in a way
that gestures toward the issues that dominated first-century debate among Christians and between Jews and Christians, and also

[1] There may be a further nuance to the name. An English transliteration of
Peter's name would be *shimon* (no Greek letter was sounded "sh"), which is

gives us his readers a clue regarding the letter's background issues.

Peter also introduces himself with two titles, "bondservant" and "apostle." While "servant" might be seen as a way of highlighting the author's humility, in many of its biblical uses it is a title of honor. Moses was the "servant of the Lord" (Josh. 14:7), as was Abraham (Ps. 105:42), Jacob (Is. 48:20), and the coming Messiah (Is. 42:1; etc.).[2] In the New Covenant, the word is used with reference to the entire church (1 Pet. 2:16), and it describes the absolute commitment required of the disciple (Gal. 1:10). As servants of God, Paul says in 1 Corinthians 4:1, the apostles are entrusted with the secret things of God. Most interesting for our purposes is the use of this word in connection with the prophets (2 Kgs. 17:23: "His servants the prophets"; cf. Mt. 21:34). Prophets were the Lord's servants who brought the Word of the Lord to His people, and in particular brought the "covenant lawsuit" that condemned Israel for her unfaithfulness. Peter is doing the same.

The Greek word for "apostle" has its roots in the Hebrew "office" of *shaliach*,[3] the office of a specially commissioned representative who acted with the full authority of the one who commissioned him. The accent of the word is on the *authority* of the messenger, not merely on the fact that he acts as a messenger.[4] New Testament usage of "apostle" carries on this note of authority. Thus, we find in Matthew 10:1–2 that the designation of the Twelve changes from

---

taken from the Hebrew verb "to hear" (*shema*). There might thus also be a veiled allusion to the confession of Yahweh in Deuteronomy 6 and an announcement that Peter's readers need to heed his own "shema." It is as if Peter were playing the part of Moses and saying, "Hear, O Israel."

[2] See also Moo, *2 Peter, Jude*, 33–34.

[3] Karl Heinrich Rengstorf, s.v. "apostolos," *Theological Dictionary of the New Testament*, ed. Gerhard Kittel, trans. Geoffrey Bromily, 10 vols. (Grand Rapids: Eerdmans, 1964), 1:413–20.

[4] As Rengstorf puts it, "the point of the designation *sheluchim* is neither description of the fact of sending nor indication of the task involved but simply assertion of the form of sending, i.e., of authorization. This is the decisive thing. The task as such is of no significance for the quality as *shalicha*" (Ibid., 415).

"disciple" to "apostle" when they are granted authority to go on a mission. Interestingly, though the word *shaliach* was not used by rabbinic Judaism to refer to the prophets, it is used of prophet Ahijah in 1 Kings 14:6.

Apostles go beyond prophets since they bear the revelation of the last days given through the Son (Heb. 1:1–3), and since they act with the full capacity of the Lord. Still, prophets and apostles are similar in various respects. In particular, like the prophets, the apostles prepare the way for the Lord's coming by presenting the covenant lawsuit against the people of God and warning them that they have broken covenant and stand in the way of God's wrath.

This has an important bearing on our interpretation of 2 Peter. Throughout the epistle, and indeed throughout the New Testament, there is a concern with an imminent "coming of the Lord." As I noted in chapter 1, I believe these prophecies refer to the coming destruction of the Temple in A.D. 70, which marked the end of the Old Creation and brought in a New Creation. Given Peter's evident concern for this future event displayed in both his letters, it is no accident that Peter introduces himself to his readers with a phrase that connotes (among other things) an authoritative and prophetic office.

Like the prophets, Peter warns of future events in order to stir people up to repentance and to urge the saints to continue in the way of holiness. He moves on from the introduction, therefore, to outline what Christian living looks like. Two issues here are relevant for our purposes: Hellenism and eschatology. First, commentators suggest that Peter writes about the Christian life under the heavy influence of Hellenistic categories, terms, and ideas, and thus 2 Peter provides an early illustration of what the liberal church historian Adolf von Harnack called the "acute Hellenization" of Christianity. I will begin by challenging that argument and showing that Peter's vision of the Christian life is thoroughly biblical, Hebraic, and consistent with Paul. Second, the overall eschatological context of Peter's letter has influenced the way he describes the Christian life. It is not a trivialization of Peter's theology to say that in 1:3–11 he is describing how people should live if they want to avoid being destroyed in the coming judgment. Below, I expand on that theme by showing how Peter's overview of the Christian life sets the stage for later portions of his letter.

"PARTAKERS OF THE DIVINE NATURE": 1:3–11

Man was created to be the image of God in that he is to reflect God's glory physically—to serve as God's viceroy over the earth by "multiplying, taking dominion, and subduing the earth," and by reflecting God's ability to create through speech in human speech and creativity. Adam was also created to be the image of God in an ethical sense: he was to be perfect, as His Father in heaven is perfect. When he sinned, Adam lost this image of God in this ethical sense; while he continued to display the beauty, creativity, and dominion of God, he displayed all this in a perverse way. Christ, the Last Adam, restored this image to all who are united to Him by faith.

This way of stating Christ's purpose in redemption is more Pauline than Petrine, but Peter is writing about the same reality, though he never uses the phrase "image of God" or refers to Adam. Instead he uses the striking and controversial phrase "partakers of the divine nature" (v. 4; *theias koinonoi phuseos*). Rather than saying that we are restored to divine "image," Peter says that we participate in divine "nature"; rather than saying we become God-*like*, Peter seems to be saying that we become gods. Though this has been one of the main pieces of evidence for the claim that 2 Peter is a "Hellenizing" letter, the idea that humans, especially rulers, are "gods" is found in the Old Testament:

> If the thief is not found, then the owner of the house shall stand before the gods (Heb. *elohim*, trans. as "judges") to determine whether he laid his hands on his neighbor's property. (Exod. 22:8)

> God takes His stand in the congregation of God; He judges in
> the midst of the gods. How long will you judge unjustly, and
> show partiality to the wicked? . . . I said, You are gods, and all of
> you are sons of the Most High. (Ps. 82:1–2, 6)

Further, in a trinitarian framework, Jesus clearly taught that
Christians enter the fellowship (*koinonia*) of Father, Son, and
Spirit: "I do not ask on behalf of these alone, but for those also who
believe in Me through their word; that they may all be one; even as
Thou, Father, art in Me, and I in Thee, that they also may be one in
Us . . . I in them, and Thou in Me, that they may be perfected in
unity" (Jn. 17:21–23).

Corroboratory evidence of Peter's concern with the restoration
of the image of God is his use of the Greek word *arete* in 2 Peter 1:3,
5. Translated as "virtue" in some versions, the word has a long history in Greek ethics and is particularly important for Aristotelian
and neo-Aristotelian ethicists. Like "partakers of divine nature,"
this word has been used as evidence for Hellenistic influences in
Peter's ethics. It is likely, however, that the term should be translated differently. In verse 3, it refers to an attribute of God in parallel with the word "glory" (Greek, *doxa*), and there the NASB
translates it as "excellence." Significantly, the word is used in
Habakkuk 3:3 (LXX) as the Greek translation of *hod*, "majesty" or
"splendor." Likewise the Septuagint of Isaiah 42:8 uses *arete* to
translate *kabod*, the normal Hebrew word for "glory" (cf. Is. 42:12
and 63:7, where *arete* has the sense of "praise"). Given this background of usage and the fact that Peter pairs *arete* with *doxa*
("glory"), it appears Hebraic wine has burst the Greek wineskin.[5]

Thus the flow of Peter's description is that God (or Jesus) has
"called us by His own glory and splendor," and as a result, we are to
be diligent to add "splendor" to our faith. The repetition of the word

[5] Bauckham (*Jude, 2 Peter*, 179) says that *arete* is a virtual equivalent of *doxa*.

in verses 3 and 5 indicates that Peter is talking about Christians displaying the glory of God in their lives. *This* is what participation in the divine nature looks like.[6]

THE ESCHATOLOGICAL STRUCTURE OF THE CHRISTIAN LIFE

Some who see 2 Peter as Hellenistic have claimed that Peter has transformed the Pauline view of the Christian life into a version of moralism. Instead of emphasizing the radically eschatological[7] character of the Christian life, it is charged, Peter just lays out a set of virtues that Christians are to be "diligent" to achieve. This is a misreading of Peter's views in a number of respects.

For starters, Peter's conception of this restoration is decidedly dynamic. Images of growth abound throughout these verses. Peter expresses the wish that grace and peace would be *multiplied* to his readers (1:2), and he describes the Christian life in terms of fruits heaped one upon another so that a picture of glorious abundance emerges (vv. 5–7). Verse 8 speaks of the fruits both belonging to his readers and increasing. Christian living is, for the aging Peter, a continuous process and advancement in holiness and "glory." The future orientation of the Christian life remains: Peter ends his list of

[6] It would be interesting, but unfortunately beyond both my time and competence, to examine recent work in "virtue ethics" (from writers like Stanley Hauerwas) with Peter's transformed use of *arete*. In particular, since virtue often has a "heroic" and even violent connotation in Greek epic and philosophy, the appeal to the crucified and risen Jesus as the source and standard of "virtue" takes us in a strikingly un-Hellenistic direction.

[7] Here "eschatological" does not have so much to do with the things that happen at the end of history but rather with the character of the New Covenant itself. Because Jesus has risen and we partake of Him, we are also, already, participants in the resurrection; we also, already, live "eschatological" lives. To be sure, the present reality of eschatological life is oriented to a future full eschatological life, but even now Christian living is a participation in the age to come.

fruits by reminding his readers that faithful practice of Christian life will ensure that the entrance into the kingdom of Christ will be abundantly supplied (v. 11). Faith grows up into love, and all is surrounded and infused with hope.

The counter-charge has been made that Peter has shunted the Christian's entrance into the life of the kingdom off into the unspecified future. Paul says that we *have been* translated into the kingdom of the Son (Col. 1:13), that whoever is in Christ is a new creation (2 Cor. 5:17), that we have been raised up to be seated in the heavenly places with Christ (Eph. 2:6). Peter, so it is argued, was so deeply influenced by the more static categories of Greek and Roman thought that he places the kingdom exclusively in the future. What has become of Paul's indicative-imperative scheme, his constant emphasis on "become what you already are"?

In reality, Peter's conception of the Christian life is as eschatologically informed and structured as Paul's, and not only in the sense that Peter sees the Christian life as a path of growth leading ultimately into the kingdom of Christ: Peter is as insistent on the "now" of Christian eschatology as Paul. Peter, first of all, grounds the Christian life in God's prior action. The verb "receive" in verse 1 emphasizes the graciousness of God's gift of faith,[8] and the tenses of the verbs in verses 3–4 emphasize Peter's belief that the Christian life grows up from something that has been completed ("has granted"). In both verses, the verbs are in the perfect tense, which

---

[8] Peter makes intriguing play with Paul's doctrine of justification by faith, with which he was deeply familiar (Gal. 2:11–21; 2 Pet. 3:14–16). Instead of saying that righteousness comes through faith, as Paul does, Peter claims that we receive "faith" through the "righteousness of our God and Savior Jesus Christ" (1:1). Many commentators say that "righteousness" is introduced here to emphasize God's impartiality in giving faith of "equal value" to both Peter and his readers. I suspect something more is going on: through Jesus' act of righteousness, His faithfulness to His Father and His faithfulness with His Father, faith is secured for His people.

in Greek carries the specific connotation of a completed action that has a continuing result. It is a finished fact that God has granted all things for life (v. 3), and Christians are now to diligently nourish what has been given. God's action is prior to and foundational for the Christian's life and godliness, so that Peter teaches, against all Greek ethics, that "glorious" or "virtuous" life is only possible by grace. Peter, as well as Paul, condemns Homer's heroes and Aristotle's self-made man.

These verses also hint that the Christian life depends specifically on participation in the death and resurrection of Christ. By "divine power," Peter says, we are granted everything necessary for life and godliness (1:3). That it takes an exertion of divine power to make us alive and godly should give us pause, but my point is elsewhere: throughout Scripture, divine power is exerted in specific historical acts (Exod. 15:6, 13; Ps. 21:13; 145:4; Lk. 4:14, 36; etc.), most centrally displayed in the raising of Jesus from the dead, which destroyed the dominion and power of death and sin (1 Cor. 6:14; 2 Cor. 13:4). In Acts 2:24, Peter himself points to the resurrection as a display of God's power over death. For Paul and indeed for all the New Testament writers, the exalted Christ *is* the power of God (1 Cor. 1:24), and the gospel of Christ is the power of God unto salvation (Rom. 1:16). The power in us who believe is resurrection power (Eph. 1:19–20).

When Peter says that life and godliness are the product of God's power, he does not have in mind some abstract, general power of God. Rather, Peter links the life and godliness that belong to the Christian with God's display of power in the resurrection of Christ. It is by virtue of our union with the resurrected Christ that we have power to produce the fruits described in verses 5–7.[9] Only by union with the eschatological "now" of Jesus' incorruptible life can we escape the corruption that is in the world (cf. v. 4). For Peter

---

[9] Moo, *2 Peter, Jude*, 41.

as much as for Paul, there are two worlds within the world: one under the dominion of sin, corruption, and death, and the other empowered by the all-triumphant resurrection power of Jesus.

This resurrection power that produces life and godliness in the Christian is mediated through the "knowledge of the one who calls us by His own glory and splendor" (v. 3, my trans.). Peter's thought here is similar to that of Paul in 2 Corinthians 4:4, 6: unbelievers have been blinded "that they might not see the light of the gospel of the glory of Christ, who is the image of God. . . . For God, who said, 'Light shall shine out of darkness,' is the One who has shone in our hearts to give the light of the knowledge of the glory of God in the face of Christ." Despite the differences in the images, both Peter and Paul tell us that it is the glory of Christ that gives us new life as it shines upon us, and both passages speak of "knowledge." Both passages describe the Christian life as a growth in Godlikeness (2 Cor. 3:18; 2 Pet. 1:4). In short, like his "beloved brother" Paul, Peter sees the Christian life as a matter of re-creation.

God not only calls us *by* His glory and splendor, but also calls us *to* His glory (1 Pet. 5:10). Being in the kingdom is the basis of the Christian life, but entry into the kingdom is also the *goal* of the Christian life (2 Pet. 1:11). Again we have a similarity with Paul, whose thought is summarized not only in the expression, "Be what you are," but also "be what you will be." What has happened to the Christian is an anticipation of what will happen to him on the last day: we have been remade in the image of Christ, and we shall be so remade; we have received an inheritance, and we shall receive an inheritance; we are partakers of divine nature, but we will become partakers.

As already noted, between the initial and final entrances into the kingdom, the Christian is called to a life of godliness and fruitfulness in the knowledge of Christ. According to Paul and Peter, this requires effort. Peter exhorts his readers to be diligent in their efforts to supply additions to their faith (v. 5). They are to "apply *all* diligence" in seeking to be fruitful in the knowledge of Christ. After warning about the dangers of shortsightedness, Peter calls his readers to be "all the *more* diligent to make certain of your calling and election" (v. 10).[10]

Like Paul, Peter structures the Christian life in a threefold time frame: what *has* happened anticipates what *will* happen, and both what has happened and what will happen condition what *is* happening and what we are to *do*. Divine power has been exerted in the resurrection of Jesus to fulfill God's promise to us; the purpose of God's action is to make us partakers of the divine nature and to ensure our glorious entrance into the kingdom. Because God has acted, and in view of what we shall become, we must be diligent in pursuing and producing the fruits of the Spirit.

This understanding of the Christian life is illustrated and summarized by baptism, which Peter alludes to by the word "purification" (v. 9). Through baptism, we enter into the new life of the Spirit, receive a grant of divine power, are incorporated into Christ's body, and die and rise again with Christ. In the purification of baptism, we are cleansed of our "former sins" (v. 9) and begin to participate in the divine nature and the power of Jesus' resurrection. But we must be diligent not to become forgetful or nearsighted (v. 9; cf. v. 4), forgetting our purification. Instead we must, as the Westminster Divines put it, "improve upon our baptism." Baptism thus marks our entrance into Christ's kingdom, points to our future entry, and demands perseverance and effort in working out our salvation with fear and trembling.

Escape from the corruption of the world (v. 4) may be related to baptism. The verb *apopheugo* is in the aorist, which frequently

[10] Again, the tense of the verbs underscores the point that Peter is making. In verse 10 the verbs are in the present tense, which in Greek frequently carries the connotation of continuous action. Peter is exhorting his readers to "keep on practicing" the fruits of the knowledge of Christ and says they must "be making" their election and choosing sure (v. 10).

(though not always) indicates a definite, once-for-all act rather than a process. Moreover, the New Testament occasionally draws an antithesis between "corruption" and "glory" (Rom. 8:21; 1 Cor. 15:42–43) and associates the "glory" specifically with the resurrection. In Galatians 6:8, Paul contrasts the reward of the fleshly man ("corruption") with the reward of the spiritual man ("eternal life"),[11] and Peter describes the pseudo-prophets as slaves of corruption (2 Pet. 2:19). Verse 4 thus describes a definitive escape from the corruption that characterizes the world; having escaped, we become partakers of the divine nature, sharers in God's glory.

Peter's description of Christian living, in short, is perfectly consistent with Paul's. To be sure, Peter uses terms that produce a series of Hellenistic echoes, but even then he has transformed the meaning of those terms in the light of biblical categories. His description of the Christian life has lost none of the eschatological edge found in Paul, a fact symbolized by Peter's decision to list *eight* products of the divine power that delivers us from the corruptions of the world——for the number eight is the number of the new creation, of the day that begins a new week, of the man that is saved from eschatological judgment (cf. 2 Pet. 2:5).[12]

ENTRANCE INTO THE KINGDOM

The exhortations of 1:1–11 are integral to the prophetic focus of Peter's letter. Seen in the context of the letter as a whole, Peter's ethical exhortations might be developed in a book entitled "How to Avoid Being Destroyed in the Coming Judgment." To show Peter's exhortation is linked to his prophetic teaching, I examine several specific terms that Peter uses in 1:3–11 and elsewhere in his letter.

---

[11] Incidentally, it might be noted that these contrasts of corruption with glory and life lend support to our interpretation of Peter's phrase "partakers of the divine nature."

[12] See J.N.D. Kelly, *A Commentary on the Epistles of Peter and Jude* (San Francisco: Harper & Row, 1969).

1. Godliness: In 1:3, 6–7, the theme of godliness is introduced. God has exerted His power to give us all we need for "life and godliness," which are not to be understood as two separate items but simply as "godly living." As noted above, God's power is given for this purpose, but this does not cancel out the need for us to pursue godliness. On the contrary, *because* God has exerted His power to give us all things pertaining to life and godliness, we should apply diligence to add one virtue on another. The central section of the letter, 2:4–10, picks up on the theme of godliness from the first section. Here the point is that the godly will be rescued from trials, while the ungodly will be destroyed: God "brought a flood on the world of the ungodly" and destroyed Sodom and Gomorrah as "an example to those who would live ungodly thereafter" (2:5–6). On the other hand, these events also demonstrate that "the Lord knows how to rescue the godly from temptation," while keeping the ungodly under punishment for a coming day of judgment (2:9). Thus, Peter's exhortation that his readers be diligent to add godliness to their perseverance (1:6) comes in the context of a promise and a warning—the promise that the godly will be rescued and the warning that the ungodly will be destroyed.

2. Promises: Peter says in 1:4 that God has fulfilled His great and precious promises to us. God exerted power to fulfill the promise that we will be made partakers of divine nature. Among the promises that God made are the promises of His coming (Greek, *parousia*; 3:4; 1:16) and of a new heavens and earth in which righteousness dwells (3:13). In short, the promise of the Parousia is one of the "great and magnificent promises," as is the promise of a new world.[13] Integral to Peter's claim that God has granted promises, and that by these promises we are restored to

---

[13] Also, the fact that God has exerted His divine power to achieve these promises means that the Parousia is also assured. It is also an exertion of divine power, for it is the "powerful coming" of Christ.

godlikeness, is the further claim that God has promised to judge and transform the heavens and earth.

3. Stability: Peter says in 1:12 that he wants to remind these Christians of things they already know. They are already "established" or "stabilized" in the truth, but they need to maintain stability. The prophecy helps them maintain stability and keeps them from stumbling and falling. We see a related word in 3:17, where Peter states that his intention is to warn his readers beforehand about what is going to happen so that they will not be upended by events or by false teachers (2:14). False teachers focus their efforts on unstable souls, people who are in danger of toppling over. They are Amalekites who prey on the weak and weary members of the church. But the false teachers cause instability or exacerbate it because they are themselves "unstable" (3:16), distorting and twisting or torturing the Scriptures. Again, Peter's concern for the "stability" of his readers is sharpened by the contemporary threat of "instability."

4. Entry into the Kingdom: Peter says at the end of his opening exhortation that those who walk in the path of faith and love and all the virtues between will "never stumble" but will instead find entry into the kingdom: "The entrance into the eternal kingdom of our Lord and Savior Jesus Christ will be abundantly supplied to you" (1:11). If we take this as a reference to the final state of the believer, there is a clear connection between Peter's ethics and his eschatological expectations: only those who live godly lives will stand in the final judgment and enter the kingdom. Justified by faith, we ultimately will be judged by works.

I do not doubt that this is part of Peter's intention, but there are reasons for suspecting that he also has in mind something that is more imminent on the horizon. In a later section of chapter 1, Peter says that he wants his readers to be "able to call these things to mind" (1:15), which in the immediate context refers to the instruction about godly living that he has offered in verses 3–11. He wants to remind them of their privileges and duties as Christians, so that

they will be able to find entry into the kingdom of Jesus (v. 11). In
verse 16, however, Peter moves into a new discussion and raises for
the first time the question of Jesus' power and coming. Though this
is a new topic, Peter connects it with the preceding discussion with
the conjunction "for" (*gar*). While the Greek conjunction can have a
number of connotations, the most common and most natural
meaning here is "for this reason" or "because." This suggests that the
topic of Jesus' coming is not really a new topic at all. Peter's insis-
tence on the reliability of this prophetic word is the basis for his
diligence to help his readers remember to pursue holiness. The
flow of the argument runs like this:

> Diligently pursue godliness,
>> So that you may enter the kingdom.
> I wrote these exhortations down so you won't forget them,
>> Because we didn't make up the story of Jesus' coming.

Motivation for pursuing godliness can be described in two ways:
"Pursue godliness, so that you may enter the kingdom of Jesus";
and, alternatively, "Pursue godliness, because Jesus is coming."

The upshot of this is that the "coming" of Jesus (1:16) and the "entry into the kingdom" (1:11) describe the same reality. Jesus'
Parousia (coming) will be at the same time the "coming of the
kingdom" in its New Covenant fullness, and *that* is the kingdom
that Peter wants his readers to enter. Like Noah and Lot (2:4–8),
the godly Christians of the first-century church will watch the
world collapse around them, and like Noah and Lot, they can be
confident God will rescue them from that collapse and will give
them entry into a new world on the other side. Thus the "kingdom
of our Lord and Savior" describes not the consummation of all
things but the world of the New Covenant. If this is an accurate interpretation of Peter's argument in chapter 1, it sets the context
for chapter 3: when Peter talks about a "new heavens and new
earth," he is talking about the "kingdom of our Lord and Savior"

which emerges from the birth pangs of Jesus' coming in power. When we consider chapter 3, this will assist us in determining the timing of the events Peter prophesies there.

"CALLING THESE THINGS TO MIND": 1:12–21

Peter, as we have seen, wrote this letter to aid his readers' memory (1:12–15). Peter's emphasis on his letter as a memorial fits with the parallel with Deuteronomy noted in the previous chapter (see footnote 20). In Deuteronomy, Moses gives Israel a "second law" that will guide them when they enter the land, and throughout Deuteronomy, Moses exhorts Israel to remember what Yahweh had done in Egypt and in the wilderness. Yahweh had made war against Egypt on Israel's behalf, and now that they are entering the land, He promises to strap on His buckler and helmet to make war against the Canaanites. Moses wants Israel to remember Yahweh's deliverance *then* in order to inspire them to diligence in war *now*:

> If you should say in your heart, "These nations are greater than I; how can I dispossess them?" you shall not be afraid of them; you shall well remember what Yahweh your God did to Pharaoh and to all Egypt: the great trials which your eyes saw and the signs and the wonders and the mighty hand and the outstretched arm by which Yahweh your God brought you out. So shall Yahweh your God do to all the peoples of whom you are afraid. (Deut. 7:17–19)

> And you shall remember all the way which Yahweh your God has led you in the wilderness these forty years, that He might humble you, testing you, to know what was in your heart. . . . (Deut. 8:2)

> Remember, do not forget, how you provoked Yahweh your God to wrath in the wilderness; from the day that you left the land of Egypt until you arrived at this place, you have been rebellious against Yahweh. (Deut. 9:7)

Deuteronomy is itself an aid to memory. When Moses had completed the book, he committed it to the care of the Levites who were to read it every seventh year at the Feast of Booths, and it was to remain beside the ark as a witness against Israel (Deut. 31:9–13, 24–29). These provisions ensured the continuity of the covenant. Deuteronomy tells how the covenant people are to be organized and how they are to live, but if this organization and life are to continue from one generation to another, the documents that govern the people have to be preserved and known. Peter has similar concerns with his "second letter"—to ensure that the next generation, which is moving out of the wilderness of the apostolic period into the promised land of the new heavens and new earth, will live righteously in the land that the Lord gives them. Further, Deuteronomy is full of prophecies of Israel's future. Moses not only lays out the law and warns Israel of the consequences of breaking covenant, but prophesies extensively of Israel's future rebellion against Torah (Deut. 27–32).[14] Again, like Moses, Peter is laying out what is going to come. Peter's anxiety to communicate with his readers arises from his circumstances: he is about to die,[15] which again matches the situation of Moses in Deuteronomy. Both the prophet and the apostle want God's people to remain faithful to their Lord after their departure.

2 Peter 1:16 gets to the heart of his reminder, which is about the

[14] This point has been developed by N. T. Wright in *The Climax of the Covenant: Christ and the Law in Pauline Theology* (Minneapolis: Fortress, 1993), especially in chapter 7.

[15] Peter uses architectural imagery to describe the last days of his life, describing his coming death as the "laying aside of my dwelling," and speaks of his life now as being "in this dwelling." The closest parallel in the New Testament is in 2 Corinthians 5, where Paul describes his present existence as being in a "tent." Here the word "tent" is explicit. But Paul tells us he is hoping for something greater, a permanent house. He does not want to be unclothed but re-clothed with a house from heaven, a weight of glory that goes beyond all he could imagine.

coming (*parousia*) of the Lord.[16] Peter's main concern is to assure his readers that the prophecy of Jesus' coming is not a fable, a "sophisticated myth." This, apparently, was exactly what his opponents were claiming: false teachers mentioned in chapters 2 and 3 said the apostles were making up the prophecies about Christ's coming. Following the legal requirements of Torah, Peter offers two witnesses to support his teaching about the "power and coming" of Jesus.

First, Peter was present at and witnessed the Transfiguration of Jesus (vv. 16–18). Like Moses, Peter was on the holy mountain, heard the voice of God, and saw the Lord's glory pass before him. Because Peter saw Jesus glorified and heard the Father's voice, he says that the prophetic word is made more sure. How does this help Peter's case? A skeptic might well say, "Even if we grant that you saw Jesus translated to glory, how does this prove that the prophecy of His coming is true?" Peter's logic is twofold:

(A) The glorification of the Son on the Mount of Transfiguration is an earnest of His glorification that will occur at the time of His "power and coming" on the "day of God." More specifically, the voice that Peter records here is quoting from Psalm 2, which is about the enthronement of the Son of Yahweh. Peter saw a glimpse of Jesus enthroned as King, and as King He will come in power, and those who are diligent will enter His kingdom. The Transfiguration is thus a preview of the Parousia of Jesus, His vindication of His people, and His vindication as King at His coming.

(B) Peter's use of the Transfiguration becomes clearer when we go back to the Gospels' account of that event. In the Synoptics, the

---

[16] "Power and coming" do not refer to two separate things. Peter frequently uses near-synonyms elsewhere in 2 Peter; e.g., 1:3 ("glory and excellence"), 1:4 ("precious and magnificent promises"), 1:8 ("neither useless nor unfruitful"), 1:9 ("blind or shortsighted"). So in verse 16 we apparently have a hendiadys—*power* and *coming* do not refer to separate events. Rather, the idea is that when the Lord Jesus comes, He will come in power.

Transfiguration comes immediately after Jesus' prophecy of a powerful coming: "Truly I say to you, there are some of those who are standing here who shall not taste death until they see the Son of Man coming in His kingdom" (Mt. 16:28, cf. Mk. 9:1; Lk. 9:27). Of course, the Gospels are not always chronologically arranged, sometimes following very different arrangements. Yet each of the synoptic writers saw fit to record the Transfiguration immediately after this prophecy. That may mean that the two events were chronologically related, but even if not, the Gospel writers certainly understood that the Transfiguration was somehow connected with the prophecy.

In the Gospels, the sequence is this: Jesus says, "I will come in power and glory while some of you still are alive," and then three of the disciples *see* His glory. This shows that Jesus was not just telling stories when He talked about His power and coming. Before Jesus comes as King, Jesus is revealed as King; at His coming He will be revealed as the Royal Son on the Holy Mountain of Zion.[17] It is surely wrong to say, as some commentators do, that the Transfiguration *is* the "coming in power" that Jesus spoke of in Mark 9:2, etc.; however, it does make sense to say that the Transfiguration is a preview, a foretaste, an earnest of the coming in power that Jesus had just (in the text if not historically) predicted. In context, the Transfiguration is not a revelation of the deity of the Son of God, nor is it a generic revelation of His royal glory. Jesus' Transfiguration had a specific purpose: it confirmed His prophecy of His own powerful coming, a coming He predicted would occur within the lifetime of His disciples. Peter's argument is the same: the Trans-

---

[17] There is a clear Sinai reference in the Transfiguration scene: Jesus, the glory glorified, was manifested; Moses appeared and Peter talked about setting up "booths" as Moses did at the foot of the mountain. Yet I agree with Moo that the reference is most especially to Zion, the "holy hill" of Psalm 2:6 (Moo, *2 Peter, Jude*, 74). This means that Jesus' Transfiguration sets Him up in direct opposition to Jerusalem and its temple.

figuration confirms that the Parousia *will* occur, since it has *already been* manifested.[18]

We can take this a step further: Jesus' prophecy of His powerful coming in Matthew 16 and its parallels is an abbreviated version of His Olivet Discourse. In both, the Son of Man is said to come (16:28; 24:3) with glory and with the hosts of angels (16:27; 24:30–31). Both foretell events that will take place before the disciples die (16:28), before "this generation" passes away (24:34).[19] Others have shown that Matthew 24, at least in verses 1–35, predicts the destruction of Jerusalem,[20] and thus if Jesus' prediction of His coming is a short statement of Matthew 24, then the Transfiguration is a preview of the glorification of the Son in His powerful coming to Jerusalem in A.D. 70. The Transfiguration manifests the glory that Jesus would display in judgment on Jerusalem.

Knock-Down Argument #2:

Peter defends the reliability of the promised coming of Jesus by reference to the Transfiguration. In each of the Synoptics, this event is connected immediately with a prophecy of Jesus' "coming" within the life-time of some of His disciples, a prophecy filled out in

---

[18] Bauckham recognizes this point, though he does not follow it, resisting the implication he admits is "apparent": "A more speculative possibility is that the saying [of Mt.] 16:28 . . . may also have been connected with the Transfiguration in the non-synoptic tradition known to 2 Peter, if it is to this saying that the phrase . . . [in 2 Pet. 1:16] alludes. This possibility should be considered with the possibility that the remarks of the scoffers (3:4) have in view that saying's apparent prediction of the Parousia within the first Christian generation" (*Jude, 2 Peter*, 210).

[19] Matthew invariably uses "this generation" to refer to the generation of Jews that witnessed the ministries of John and Jesus (Mt. 3:7; 11:16; 12:34, 39, 41–42, 45; 16:4; 17:17; 23:33, 36).

[20] See, e.g., J. Marcellus Kik, *An Eschatology of Victory* (Phillipsburg, N. J.: Presbyterian and Reformed, 1971).

the Olivet Discourse. Peter's argument from the Transfiguration makes best sense if he is using it to support this prophecy. Thus the "coming" that Peter insists will happen is an event that Jesus said would take place in the first century.

If the knock-down argument in the previous chapter was merely a hard jab, this one is an uppercut, and I think it connected: I saw his knees buckle.

Peter's entire letter grows out of a dispute over the prophecy of the "power and coming" of Jesus, a prophecy uttered just before the Transfiguration. Jesus placed a clear time limit on that power and coming: a time before some standing with him tasted death. When Peter says in verse 19 that "we have the prophetic word made sure," he is talking about this *specific* prophetic word, not *generic* prophecy. If, as most commentators believe, "the prophetic word" refers to Old Testament prophecy in general, or the entire Old Testament as prophecy, then the link with the Transfiguration is much looser. How would the Transfiguration make Old Testament prophecy "more sure," or give us a firmer hold on it?[21] We simply will not understand the debate between Peter and his opponents if we fail to see that Peter is talking about *this* prophecy.[22]

Similarly, the description of the prophetic word as "a lamp shining in a dark place, until the day dawns" (v. 19) also makes best sense

---

[21] It is plausible that the Transfiguration confirmed prophecies from the OT about the Parousia of Yahweh, but these prophecies are given a specific focus in Jesus' own prophecy that He uttered just prior to His Transfiguration.

[22] This becomes all the more provocative if Michael Goulder is correct that the Synoptics intended the Transfiguration pericope to be associated with the feast of Dedication. Jesus' prediction of the end of the temple, thus, was read during the liturgical remembrance of the renewal of the temple under the Maccabees. See Goulder, *The Evangelists' Calendar: A Lectionary Explanation of the Development of Scripture* (London: SPCK, 1978), 89–90.

as a description of the prophecy of Jesus' power and coming, spoken by Jesus Himself. The coming "day" and the "rising of the morning star" refers to Jesus' coming in His kingdom within the generation of His disciples. In a dark generation such as the one that Peter lives in, the prophetic hope is the only spark of day his readers have, and they hold to it and walk by its light until the day dawns. When day dawns, lamps are put out. When Jesus makes good on His promise to avenge the blood of His saints, then the prophecy is fulfilled and the day dawns in full. If, on the other hand, "day" refers to the final judgment and the resurrection, then Peter is describing the entire New Covenant period as a period of darkness, in which the one lonely light is the prophecy of Jesus' coming, but this hardly does justice to the gospel proclamation that Jesus is the "light that has come into the world."

Douglas Moo gets half the point of this passage:

> . . . [T]he Transfiguration experience had an intimate relationship to the Parousia of Jesus.
>   We find a number of pointers in this direction. (1) The Synoptic Gospels preface the Transfiguration narrative with Jesus' prediction that some of the apostles would not die before they saw the glory of the kingdom (Mt. 17:1; Mk. 9:1; Lk. 9:27). The most natural interpretation is to find this prediction fulfilled in the Transfiguration, when only a few of the apostles (Peter, James, and John) saw Jesus' intrinsic glory.[23]

Moo is correct that the Transfiguration reveals the glory that will be revealed at the Parousia, but it is utterly nonsensical for Jesus to tell His disciples that "some" will not die before they see the glory of Jesus, if in fact that glory is going to be revealed only six or eight days later. Jesus must be referring to some other revelation of His glory, of which the Transfiguration is a proleptic sign.

---

[23] *2 Peter, Jude,* 74.

Bauckham rightly emphasizes that the Transfiguration and Peter's treatment of it depict Jesus as the Last Adam, fulfilling the promise of Psalm 8 and Daniel 7 about a new Man who will exercise universal dominion.[24] Here again, however, the Transfiguration is directly connected to prophecies of the fall of Jerusalem and the Old Covenant. According to Revelation, it is only when the harlot Jerusalem, the "great city" (Rev. 11:8; 17:18) has been destroyed that the hosts of heaven sing their climactic song: "Hallelujah! For the Lord our God, the Almighty, reigns. Let us rejoice and be glad and give the glory to Him, for the marriage of the Lamb has come and His bride has made herself ready" (Rev. 19:6b–7). Christ's reign as New Adam began with the Resurrection, began with the Ascension, began with Pentecost; and it also began with the overthrow of the harlot and the beginning of a New Creation.

ORIGIN OF PROPHECY

If Peter's first witness against the mockers is specific, the second witness is the more general statement that no prophecy is from an act of human will.[25] This is not, as so often interpreted, a statement about hermeneutics. As many commentators recognize, Peter is concerned about the origin of Scripture, which is found in the Holy Spirit not in the human will or in one's own "interpretation." Prophecy is not based on one's reflection on human history but comes from God. Because, like other prophecies of Scripture, the prophecy of the coming of Jesus comes from the Holy Spirit, it is reliable and neither a "sophisticated myth" nor the result of Peter's own attempts to unravel the mysteries of the universe.

[24] Bauckham, *Jude, 2 Peter*, 218–219.

[25] This is not a continuation of the same argument from the Transfiguration and the "prophetic word" of Jesus. In 2 Pet. 1:20, Peter writes, "know this first of all." This phrase is also used in 3:3, where it clearly introduces a new subject, the mockers. In 1:20 it serves the same function of introducing a separate line of argument.

This argument only works if the prophecy that Peter has taught his readers is on the same level as "Scripture." In fact, Peter's argument falls apart unless he is talking about a prophecy that is *already* inscripturated. Peter could say, "No prophecy of Scripture is a matter of one's own interpretation," and the response would be, "Sure, but what you're talking about is not a prophecy of Scripture." Peter thus must be referring to the prophetic word of Jesus recorded in the Gospels as a prophecy of "Scripture." And that means that the Gospels *must* have been already written by this time. Supposing that Peter died sometime in the mid-60s, at least one of the Gospels must have been written and circulated as Scripture in the early 60s or the 50s. This chronology goes contrary to the consensus even among evangelical scholars, but the reasoning seems sound to me.[26]

[26] For a defense of early dating of the synoptic Gospels, see John Wenham, *Redating Matthew, Mark, and Luke: A Fresh Assault on the Synoptic Problem* (Downers Grove, Ill.: InterVarsity, 1992). I go further than Wenham, who believes in Matthean priority and who dates Matthew in the 40s. I see no reason why Matthew would have waited a decade before writing his Gospel. In fact, the idea that a Jew would wait a decade to record the climactic act of Israel's history borders on absurdity; the widespread notion that he should wait half a century is far past the border.

3
FALSE TEACHERS AMONG YOU

As we have seen, 2 Peter is a follow-up letter to 1 Peter in which Peter reminds his readers of things he has already taught them. Through this second letter, he helps them anticipate what is ahead and to handle it faithfully (2 Pet. 3:17). One of the main threats facing Peter's readers is the emergence of false teachers, and refuting the false teachers becomes the focus of his attention throughout chapter 2 and into chapter 3. "Refuting," though, is not quite the word for Peter's language; pummeling, denouncing, castigating, condemning, attacking, and assaulting are more accurate descriptions of what Peter does to his opponents. He offers a few arguments in response to false teaching in chapter 3, but chapter 2 is mainly occupied not with refutation but denunciation of the most severe sort. This chapter contains some of the harshest rhetoric in the New Testament. Peter does not think the false teachers have an argument that needs to be considered carefully and responded to point-by-point; he does not try to be balanced or "fair." Though the chapter is alarming to modern sensibilities, Peter's vehemence is just the outgrowth of his deep pastoral commitment—when he looks at the false teachers, he sees nothing but a blur of white fangs, claws, and gray fur beneath the covering of wool, and he girds himself to make war on the wolves.

Though Peter puts this pastoral denunciation at the center of his letter, he has not forgotten his main purpose in writing, which is to remind his readers of prophecies. False teachers, as well as apostasy, are a fixture in New Testament portraits of the "last days" and are intimately connected with Jesus' "power and coming." Both Jesus and Paul warn that false prophets will arise in the last days to lead many away. In His Olivet Discourse, Jesus predicted not only the presence of false prophets but their effectiveness:

> Many false prophets will arise, and will mislead many. . . . And unless those days had been cut short, no life would have been saved; but for the sake of the elect those days shall be cut short. Then if anyone says to you, "Behold, here is the Christ," or "There," do not believe. For false Christs and false prophets will arise and will show great signs and wonders, so as to mislead, if possible, even the elect. Behold, I have told you in advance. (Mt. 24:11, 22–25)

The appearance of false prophets and the beginning of apostasy are signs that Jesus' prophecy is nearing complete fulfillment. Wars and rumors of war, famine and earthquake, are just the "beginning of birth pangs" (Mt. 24:4–8), but when "tribulation" begins and "false prophets" arise, things are approaching "the end" (24:9–14). False prophets and teachers are a sign that the world is moving from early labor through transition and is about to give birth.

In His Olivet Discourse, interestingly, Jesus speaks specifically of the circumstances Peter is addressing—the consequences of an apparent delay in Jesus' coming: "If that evil slave says in his heart, 'My master is not coming for a long time, and shall begin to beat his fellow slaves and eat and drink with drunkards, the master of that slave will come when he does not expect him and at the hour which he does not know" (Mt. 24:48–50). Jesus goes on to say that such abusive slaves will be "cut in pieces" and sent to a place of "weeping . . . and gnashing of teeth" (v. 51). Like Jesus, Peter denounces the servants of Jesus who conclude "My master is not coming for a long time" and abuse the church, "denying the Master who bought them" (2 Pet. 2:1). Paul's letters to Timothy echo this theme:

> But the Spirit explicitly says that in later times some will fall away from the faith, paying attention to deceitful spirits and doctrines of demons, by means of hypocrisy of liars seared in their own conscience as with a branding iron, men who forbid marriage and advocate abstaining from foods, which God has created to be gratefully shared in by those who believe and know the truth. (1 Tim. 4:1–3)

> But realize this, that in the last days difficult times will come. . . . among them are those who enter into households and captivate weak women weighed down with sins, led on by various impulses, always learning and never able to come to the knowledge of the truth. And just as Jannes and Jambres opposed Moses, so these men also oppose the truth, men of depraved mind, rejected as regards the faith . . . . evil men and imposters will proceed from bad to worse, deceiving and being deceived. (2 Tim. 3:1, 6–8, 13)

In Revelation 13, John sees a beast come from the land (of Israel), who performs signs and wonders to lead the people of the land (of Israel) to worship the beast from the sea (of Gentiles):

> And I saw another beast coming up out of the earth; and he had two horns like a lamb, and he spoke as a dragon. And he exercises all the authority of the first beast in his presence. And he makes the earth and those who dwell in it to worship the first beast, whose fatal wound was healed. And he performs great signs, so that he even makes fire come down out of heaven to the earth in the presence of men [cf. Rev. 11:5]. And he deceives those who dwell on the earth because of the signs which it was given him to perform in the presence of the beast. (Rev. 13:11–14a)

This land beast is later identified as a "false prophet" (16:13; 19:20), who allies with the sea beast to make war against the saints.

In short, the prediction of false teachers and apostasy (including abandonment of Christian morality) is a constant in the apostolic account of the "last days." Thus Peter can say that he is telling his readers what they already know from other apostles, especially Paul (3:2, 15–16). Peter's description of the false teachers includes some unique elements, however, so we now turn to chapter 2.[1]

"SONS OF BALAAM": 2:1–3, 10b–18

Peter begins by drawing an analogy between the situation of Old Testament Israel and that of the New Testament church.[2] He assumes a typological relationship between the history of Israel and the history of the body of Christ, so that, like Paul, he believes that "these things were written for our instruction, on whom the ends of the ages have come" (1 Cor. 10:11). Does Peter have a particular series of Old Testament events in mind? If so, what period of Israel's history is it? He mentions Balaam in verse 15, so at least he evokes Israel's wilderness period.[3] This makes sense at a number of levels: Peter has taken the stance of Moses in Deuteronomy, writing a "second letter" as he nears his death, and like Moses he reminds the church of Israel's rebellion in the wilderness and the threat posed

---

[1] 2 Peter 2 can be seen as a simple chiasm, though the following outline disrupts somewhat the overall outline of the book provided in chapter 1.
  A. 2:1–3 are framed by "destruction"
  B. vv. 4–11 are framed by references to angels
  B'. vv. 12–16 are framed by *alogos zoos* and the "dumb donkey" (in their greed, these prophets have become worse than dumb animals)
  A'. vv. 17–22: these animals return to their mire (also the denial of the Lord/Master, v. 1)

[2] Peter evidently shares Paul's "ecclesiocentric" hermeneutic, which emphasizes the continuity between Israel and the church. See Ricard Hays, *Echoes of Scripture in the Letters of Paul* (New Haven:Yale, 1989).

[3] Along similar lines, Jude 11 compares the false teachers with those who perished in the rebellion of Korah.

by Balaam (cf. Deut. 9:7–21; 23:4–5). Describing the forty-year apostolic period (30–70 A.D.) as a recapitulation of the wilderness wanderings of Israel, furthermore, is consistent with other New Testament writings, particularly Hebrews.

In the Septuagint, however, nearly all the uses of the word "false prophet" (*pseudoprophetes*) are in Jeremiah (the only exception in Zech. 13:2), and the contest between true and false prophecy was one of the main issues of Jeremiah's ministry (like Elijah's before him). Jeremiah's description of false prophets matches Peter's description of false teachers on a number of points. According to Jeremiah, false prophets are greedy for gain, so they prophesy peace for a fee, though there is no peace (Jer. 6:13). When Jeremiah prophesies against the temple, foretelling that it will be destroyed like Shiloh, the false prophets charge him with a capital crime for blaspheming Yahweh's house (Jer. 26). Later the false prophets assure the people of Jerusalem that Yahweh will deliver the city from Nebuchadnezzar, but Jeremiah assures them that Nebuchadnezzar will conquer them and put them beneath his yoke. False prophets counsel resistance to the imperial power, while Jeremiah urges Israel to submit to the new world order (Jer. 27:9ff). Hananiah dramatizes the view of the false prophets by breaking the yoke that Jeremiah has been wearing, signifying that he expects Yahweh to break the yoke of the king of Babylon. Jeremiah responds by insisting that if Israel breaks the yoke of wood they will be saddled with a yoke of iron (28:1ff., especially v. 13).

According to a preterist interpretation of 2 Peter, the allusion to Jeremiah is most apt. In Jeremiah's time, as in the first century, an imperial power threatens Jerusalem and Judah. Faithful prophets and apostles warn Israel about the costs of resistance, counsel submission rather than rebellion, and insist that, whatever the appearances to the contrary, judgment is going to fall, and that right soon. False prophets and teachers, by contrast, say that the world will continue to go on as it always has. They prophesy continuity and peace. "Nebuchadnezzar," they believe, will be turned back, and the Lord will deliver Israel. Peter thus puts the false teachers in the same category as the blind guides of Jeremiah's day, and this implies that they will be soon removed. Hananiah's punishment came within the year after he broke the yoke of Jeremiah (Jer. 28:17). What hope, then, do the false teachers have?

Allusions to Jeremiah's situation in 2 Peter 2 suggest that the "false prophets" or "false teachers" arise among Jewish believers. Jesus and John both warned of false prophets arising from the "land" of Israel. Peter says as much in 2:1 ("there will also be false teachers *among you*"), and I have argued that Peter is writing to a predominantly Jewish audience (see chapter 1). This might give us a clue to the content of their false teaching, their "destructive heresies" (2 Pet. 2:1). Since the false teachers of 2:1 are the same as the "mockers" of 3:3, it is clear that the false teachers doubt the "promise of [Jesus'] coming" (3:3), apparently charging Peter and the other apostles with concocting "sophisticated myths" about an imminent judgment on the Old Creation (1:16). Peter's typological connection between Israel's history and the church's puts this skepticism in an ironic light: the mockery of the false teachers is a fulfillment of prophecy; their very existence refutes them.[4]

Yet, if they are *Jewish* false teachers, we can surmise something more about the content of their teaching. There are a number of reasons for believing that Peter's opponents are either Judaizers, Jewish believers within the church who want to stuff the New Covenant into Old Covenant wineskins, or Jewish Christians who have abandoned Christ to return to Judaism outright. Several lines

---

[4] Peter's statements about false teachers are in the future tense in 2:1–3 and 3:2. However, the future tenses are interwoven with present tenses in 2:10–22. Peter is not talking about a phenomenon that is strictly and completely future. False prophets appear in the last days, but these are already beginning. His use of the future might be explained by the fact that he is citing prophecies that were expressed in the future tense.

of evidence lead to this conclusion. First, there is the general fact that the main threat to Christianity in the first century came from Judaism. Most of the persecution recorded in the book of Acts comes at the hands of Jews, rather than Romans, and Peter is describing teachers who not only mislead but persecute the faithful.[5] In Paul's ministry, the main threat to the purity of the gospel came from Judaizers and Jews.[6] To be more specific, Peter is dealing with apostates: the false teachers "deny the Master who bought them" (2 Pet. 2:1), and having escaped the "defilements of the world by the knowledge of the Lord and Savior Jesus Christ," they now "are again entangled in them and are overcome" (v. 20). Throughout the New Testament, however, the great apostasy was not reversion to paganism but reversion to Judaism. Especially under threat of persecution, many believers found a safe haven in Judaism, which was recognized as a legal religion in the first century, and this problem is addressed extensively in the letter to the Hebrews. Thus it is *prima facie* plausible that Peter is dealing with similar opponents.

[5] Peter says that the false teachers "entice unstable souls," and the verb here is a fishing or hunting term that indicates the false teachers prey on the church. See the brief comments of Bauckham, *Jude, 2 Peter,* 266–267. Hillyer (*2 Peter, Jude,* 214) points out that the language for scoffing in 2 Peter 3 carries connotation of physical oppression (cf. Exod. 1:13; Lev. 25:43, 46), which fits with the parable of Jesus about the servant who thinks his master is delayed and decides to take advantage of the situation.

[6] If I made a fuller analysis of the opposition to the early church, I would note several stages similar to those in Revelation 12–15. First, Satan attempts directly to kill the infant Jesus and the infant church; then, Satan attempts to corrupt the church with the bitter water of false Judaizing doctrine; having failed, he raises up a sea beast (Rome) and a land beast (Jews) who together make war on the saints, particularly the hundred and forty-four thousand Jewish believers marked for martyrdom. By the time Peter is writing 2 Peter, the alliance of sea beast and land beast is in place, with Nero and the Jews together striving to destroy the church. For somewhat fuller discussion, see James Jordan's *Brief Reader's Guide to Revelation* (Niceville, Fla.: Transfiguration Press, 1999).

The fact that the false teachers show some signs of Hellenic influence does not refute this conclusion. One particular example is Peter's emphasis on "knowledge" (1:2, 3, 6, etc.), which has often been taken as evidence that he adopted the rhetorical strategy of using his opponents terminology against them and has led many to consider Peter's opponents to be "gnostics." But gnostic elements were evident in first-century Judaism, and Christian gnosticism likely developed from Jewish sects.[7] Bauckham has noted that "The author of 2 Peter was doubtless aware of the currency of these ideas [i.e., divinization, etc.] in the Hellenistic religious world, but he was probably more immediately dependent on the literature of Hellenistic Judaism, which had already adapted the terminology of Greek religion and philosophy in order to express its own religious tradition in terms appropriate to its Hellenistic environment."[8]

Second, several of the specific ways that Peter describes his opponents suggest that they are Jews. This is not always evident on the surface of the text, but when Peter's language is examined in the context of New Testament usage in general, it becomes more plausible. Several specific items may be noted:

1. Peter refers to several Old Testament events to assure his readers that the Lord will protect them in the midst of the judgment (2:4–9). The argument functions as follows: Just as the Lord spared Noah in the midst of the flood and Lot in the midst of the destruction of Sodom, so He will spare the righteous in the midst of the destruction of the "present heavens and earth" (cf. 3:7). This section thus draws analogies between Peter's own time and the two great judgments in Genesis.

Within the New Testament, these Old Testament events are commonly cited as types of the coming devastation of Jerusalem

---

[7] See the brief comments of James M. Robinson in his editor's introduction to *The Nag Hammadi Library*, rev. ed. (San Francisco: Harper and Row, 1988), 6–7.

[8] Bauckham, *Jude, 2 Peter*, 180. Bauckham provides many examples of Hellenistic ideas in Judaism.

and Judaism. Having intermarried and committed spiritual adultery with the "daughters of men" (Gentiles), the "sons of God" (Jews) have filled the land with violence and continuous evil, and can only expect to be flooded into oblivion.[9] Refusing to receive the Angel of the Lord and instead seeking to "rape" Him, the Jews had become Sodomites and could only expect to be destroyed by fire from the sky. Describing the coming destruction of apostate Israel, Jesus said that "the coming of the Son of Man will be just like the days of Noah" in its suddenness (Mt. 24:37). Luke's record of this statement makes it more obvious that this "flood" will come within the generation of the apostles:

> For just as the lightning, when it flashes out of one part of heaven, shines to the other part of heaven, so will the Son of Man be in his day. But first He must suffer many things and be rejected by this generation. And just as it happened in the days of Noah, so it shall be also in the days of the Son of Man: they were eating and drinking, they were marrying, they were being given in marriage, until the day that Noah entered the ark, and the flood came and destroyed them all. (Lk. 17:24–27)

Jesus applied flood imagery to the destruction of the city of Jerusalem, the temple, and the entire world order of which Jerusalem was the center.

Similarly, Jesus compared the destruction of Sodom to the coming destruction of the city and temple:

> It was the same as happened in the days of Lot: they were eating, they were drinking, they were buying, they were selling, they were planting, they were building; but on the day that Lot went

---

[9] One dimension of this "intermarriage" was the Jews' habit of employing methods of force and violence to resist the pagan force and violence of Rome. N.T. Wright has argued that this was a sign of the Jews' adoption of pagan political attitudes and methods.

out from Sodom it rained fire and brimstone from heaven and destroyed them all. It will be just the same on the day that the Son of Man is revealed. (Lk. 17:28–29)

In Revelation 11:8, John states explicitly that the city which is mystically known as Sodom and Egypt is the city where Jesus was crucified.

In drawing analogies between the flood, the destruction of Sodom, and a devastating judgment on Israel, Jesus, John, and Peter were drawing on a recognized thread of prophetic imagery:

Your land is desolate, your cities are burned with fire, your fields—strangers are devouring them in your presence; it is desolation, as overthrown by strangers. And the daughter Zion is left like a shelter in a vineyard, like a watchman's hut in a cucumber field, like a besieged city. Unless Yahweh of hosts had left us a few survivors, we would be like Sodom, we would be like Gomorrah. Hear the word of Yahweh, you rulers of Sodom; give ear to the instruction of our God, You people of Gomorrah. (Is. 1:7–10)

Jerusalem has stumbled, and Judah has fallen, because their speech and their actions are against Yahweh, to rebel against His glorious presence. The expression of their faces bears witness against them. And they display their sin like Sodom; they do not even conceal it. (Is. 3:8–9a)

Among the prophets of Jerusalem I have seen a horrible thing; the committing of adultery and walking in falsehood; and they strengthen the hands of evildoers, so that no one has turned back from his wickedness. All of them have become to Me like Sodom, and her inhabitants like Gomorrah. (Jer. 23:14)

For the iniquity of the daughter of my people is greater than the sin of Sodom, which was overthrown as in a moment, and no hands were turned toward her. (Lam. 4:6)

> Now your older sister is Samaria, who lives north of you with
> her daughters, and your younger sister, who lives south of you, is
> Sodom with her daughters. (Ezek. 16:46; cf. vv. 48–49, 55–56)

In a few prophesies, a Gentile city is compared to Sodom (Babylon
in Is. 13:19 and Jer. 50:40; Edom in Jer. 49:18), but predominantly
the prophets use Sodom as a type of apostate Jerusalem. Picking up
on this connection, Jesus and the apostles describe Jerusalem as if it
were a composite of all the wicked cities of biblical history (see esp.
Rev. 18). When Jesus and the apostles begin to use this terminology, they have a consistent prophetic witness behind them.

The prophets employed flood imagery in a similar manner:

> Woe to the proud crown of the drunkards of Ephraim, and to
> the fading flower of its glorious beauty, which is as the head of
> the fertile valley of those who are overcome with wine! Be-
> hold, Yahweh has a strong and mighty agent; as a storm of hail, a
> tempest of destruction, like a storm of mighty overflowing wa-
> ters, He has cast it down to the earth with His hand. (Is. 28:1–2)

> Then after the sixty-two weeks the Messiah will be cut off and
> have nothing, and the people of the prince who is to come will
> destroy the city and the sanctuary. And its end will come with a
> flood; even to the end there will be war; desolations are deter-
> mined. (Dan. 9:26)

Daniel 9:26 is particularly important, since it directly applies the
flood imagery to the destruction of the "city and the sanctuary" that
will occur after the Messiah has been cut off and after the seventy
weeks of years have reached completion.[10]

2. The reference to Balaam is also noteworthy, since the notion of

---

[10] In Nahum, flood imagery is used to describe the judgment on the apostate
city of Nineveh: "[W]ith an overwhelming flood He will make a complete end
of its site, and will pursue His enemies into darkness" (1:8).

a "Balaamite heresy" is used elsewhere in the New Testament to describe Judaizers and their teaching. Balaam is mentioned in the New Testament only in 2 Peter 2:15, Jude 11, and Revelation 2:14. The last of these is the most important for our purposes. Revelation 2:14 is part of the letter of Jesus to the church at Pergamum, where false teachers are compared to Balaam who "kept teaching Balak to put a stumbling block before the sons of Israel, to eat things sacrificed to idols, and to commit acts of immorality."

There are several reasons for taking this as a cryptic description of Judaizing. First, despite variations in terminology, the enemies of the seven churches all promote the same basic heresy. In some of the letters, such as those to Smyrna and Philadelphia, the fact that the opponents are Jewish is explicit. They claim to be Jews but are not, and Jesus describes them instead as "synagogues of Satan" (Rev. 2:9; 3:9). Arguably, too, the "false apostles" mentioned in the letter to Ephesus (Rev. 2:2) are Judaizers (compare vv. 4 and 13 of 2 Cor. 11). Those who follow "Balaam" teach the same things as those who follow "Jezebel":

> Balaam . . . kept teaching Balak to put a stumbling block before the sons of Israel, to eat things sacrificed to idols, and to commit acts of immorality. . . . [Y]ou tolerate that woman Jezebel, who calls herself a prophetess, and she teaches and leads My bond servants astray, so that they commit acts of immorality and eat things sacrificed to idols. (Rev. 2:14, 20)

In Revelation, "Jezebel" is Jerusalem, the harlot city that is leading the Christians astray, tempting them to revert to Judaism rather than face the challenge of living as a Christian in a hostile generation. "Balaam," teaching the same things, is of the same school, among the "children" of the harlot.[11]

---

[11] According to Revelation 2:14, Balaam put a "stumbling block" (*skandalon*) before the sons of Israel; presumably the new Balaamites are also putting

The two specific teachings attributed to Jezebel and Balaam—participating in idolatrous feasts and sexual immorality—do not, at first blush, sound Jewish. Within Revelation, however, "immorality" (Greek, *porneia*) always connotes spiritual adultery and is chiefly exemplified by the harlot (Greek, *porne*) Jerusalem (Rev. 14:8; 17:2, 4; 18:3; 19:2, 9). It is hardly surprising that the harlot's children would be guilty of similar immorality. Idolatry is also commonly charged against the Jews in the New Testament (e.g., Rom. 1:18–32; 2:17–24), and in Revelation the "people of the land" (Jews) are described as paying homage to the imperial beast, led on by the false prophet (Rev. 13:11–17).

There also appears to be a veiled reference to the decision of the council of Jerusalem in the descriptions of the churches' opponents in Revelation. At the council, the elders and apostles decided that they would not impose the ceremonies of the law on Gentile believers beyond the prohibitions required of Gentiles in the Old Covenant: "that you abstain from things sacrificed to idols and from blood and from things strangled and from fornication" (Acts 15:29). When Jesus says in His letters to the churches that Jezebel and Balaam and the false Jews are encouraging Christians to "eat things sacrificed to idols" and to "fornicate," He is saying that they are violating the terms of the Jerusalem Council. In short, this is a provocative way of saying that they are Judaizers.[12]

---

stumbling blocks before Christians. This seems consistent with the way that Judaizers are presented elsewhere in the New Testament. The cross is a scandal to the Jews (1 Cor. 1:23; Gal. 5:11), and in an ironic reversal of this, the Jews become a stumbling block to Christians. Specifically, Judaizers become a stumbling block for Gentile believers by trying to lay illegitimate burdens on the Gentiles.

[12] My student Richard Gall has pointed out that these two sins—idolatry and sexual immorality—are among the sins that pollute the land and cause it to spew the people out. Doubtless Jesus is making the same point about "Jezebel," "Balaam," and all the rest: they will be vomited from the land. For more, see Jonathan Klawans, *Impurity and Sin in Ancient Judaism* (Oxford: Oxford Univ. Press, 2000).

Against this background, Peter's charge that the false prophets engaged in sensuality, reveling, and greed takes on a metaphorical coloration. It is likely that Peter was charging false prophets with literal violations of the Ten Commandments, but in the New Testament these sins are related to Judaizing and Judaism. Again, Peter is picking up on a common prophetic theme, which employs shocking language of sexual infidelity to describe idolatry and apostasy. Ezekiel 16 is one of the most explicit passages:

> You trusted in your beauty and played the harlot because of your fame, and you poured out your harlotries on every passer-by who might be willing. . . . You built yourself a high place at the top of every street, and made your beauty abominable; and you spread your legs to every passer-by to multiply your harlotry. . . . Moreover, you played the harlot with the Assyrians because you were not satisfied; you even played the harlot with them and still were not satisfied. (Ezek. 16:15, 25, 28)

Compared with Ezekiel, Peter's charge that the false teachers indulge in "sensuality" seems pretty mild.

3. In 2:14, Peter describes the false teachers as "cursed children." Though the word *katara* can carry a more general connotation, it is used in the New Testament to describe the curse on those who are under the law, that is, Jews:

> For as many as are of the works of the Law are under a curse; for it is written, "Cursed is everyone who does not abide by all the things written in the Book of the Law, to perform them." . . . Christ redeemed us from the curse of the Law, having become a curse for us. . . . (Gal. 3:10–13)[13]

---

[13] Though this passage has historically been taken as a general description of the fallen and cursed state of humanity, it is clear in context that Paul is talking about a curse specific to the children of Abraham. See Richard Hays,

Likewise, Paul uses a similar phrase, "children of wrath," to describe the condition of Jews, who, he says, are as much under wrath as Gentiles (Eph. 2:3).[14]

4. Twice Peter charges the false teachers with "fleshliness" and indulgence in the "lusts of the flesh" (2 Pet. 2:10, 18). Modern readers tend to interpret "flesh" as "bodily appetites," especially sexual desires, but "flesh" normally has a very different connotation in the New Testament. On the one hand, it describes the condition of all men in Adam and indeed the entire Old Covenant order, which is a fleshly order in contrast to the New Covenant order of the Spirit.[15] More specifically, Paul frequently connects the "flesh" of circumcision with the "fleshly" interests of the Jews. Judaizers want to be perfected by the flesh (Gal. 3:3) and insist that Gentiles can be perfected only through the fleshly rite of circumcision (Gal. 5:13). Obsession with a ritual that is quite literally "fleshly" is connected with the "fleshly" behavior described in Galatians 5:19–21. When we read the list of the "works of the flesh," we cannot forget that Paul has consistently been describing the Jews and Judaizers as "fleshly." The "works of the flesh," appalling as they might be, are primarily descriptions of the behavior of Judaizers.

Paul, along similar lines, includes not only circumcision, but his entire training as a Pharisee, under the advantages of the "flesh"

Galatians, vol. 11 of *The New Interpreter's Bible*, 12 vols., ed. by Leander Keck, et. al. (Nashville: Abingdon Press, 2000), 257–262.

[14] Again, this phrase is often taken as a general description of humanity under the dominion of sin, but Paul distinguishes in Ephesians 2 between the "we" (Jews) who formerly walked in the lusts of flesh (v. 2) and the "you" (Gentiles) who, once excluded, are now brought near (vv. 11ff.).

[15] On "flesh" and "Spirit" in Paul's theology, Herman Ridderbos, *Paul: An Outline of His Theology*, trans. John Richard De Witt (Grand Rapids: Eerdmans, 1975), 64–68, is a good place to start, though Ridderbos should be supplemented by recent work that highlights the "sociological" dimension of flesh, such as James D. G. Dunn, *The Theology of Paul the Apostle* (Grand Rapids: Eerdmans, 1998), 62–70.

(Phil. 3:4–6). An even more direct analogy with Peter's usage is found in Ephesians 2:3, where Paul admits that Jews "all formerly lived in the lusts of our flesh, indulging the desires of the flesh and of the thoughts," along with Gentiles. When Peter describes the "fleshliness" of his opponents, he is employing Pauline language to describe Jews.

5. Commentators commonly note that 2 Peter 2:20 alludes to Jesus' statement in Matthew 12:43–45:[16]

> For if after they have escaped the defilements of the world by the knowledge of the Lord and Savior Jesus Christ, they are again entangled in them and are overcome, the last state has become worse for them than the first. (2 Pet. 2:20)

> Now when the unclean spirit goes out of a man, it passes through waterless places, seeking rest, and does not find it. Then it says, "I will return to my house from which I came"; and when it comes, it finds it unoccupied, swept and put in order. Then it goes, and takes along with it seven other spirits more wicked than itself, and they go in and live there; and the last state of that man shall be worse than the first. (Mt. 12:43–45)

Commentators commonly fail to note, however, that Jesus' parable is explicitly about the Jews of His own time: "That is the way it will also be with this evil generation" (Mt. 12:45). The parable comes at the end of a discussion that begins with the Pharisees claiming that Jesus is casting out demons by the power of Beelzebub. Jesus has come to exorcize the "house" of Israel, but since they do not receive Him, other demons will take up residence there.[17] When Peter alludes to this parable, he is applying it to the same cast of characters: "This perverse generation" will be worse off for hav-

---

[16] For example, Hillyer, *1 and 2 Peter, Jude*, 107.
[17] See N. T. Wright, *Jesus and the Victory of God* (London: SPCK, 1996), 455–456.

ing "escaped from the defilements of the world" only to become "again entangled in them and overcome" (2 Pet. 2:20).

Having expounded on this point for several pages, I should add that my preterist reading of 2 Peter does not depend on the above analysis of Peter's opponents. Peter's "false teachers" could well be Gentile Epicureans or Cypriat Nietzscheans or Sudanese Freedom Fighters who deny the coming of Jesus, and this does not damage the rest of my interpretation. I believe, however, that recognizing the Jewish character of Peter's opponents strengthens the preterist reading and also makes the most sense in the overall context of first-century Christianity.

POLLUTION AND EXODUS

If Peter is indeed condemning Judaizers and Jewish opponents of Christianity, his descriptions of them are sharply ironic. Reversion to the "world" (2:20) is a reversion to the world of the Old Covenant order, to a world of corruption that is about to be destroyed, to the practices and life of the "fleshly" covenant of the Jews. And the way that Peter describes the condition of this world is a direct assault on the Jews' conception of themselves. Jews were finicky about cleanliness and avoiding contamination, but Peter describes them as being full of corruption (*phthora*, vv. 12, 19; cf. 1:4) and pollution (*miasma*, v. 20). The latter word is used in the Septuagint translation of Leviticus 7:18 (LXX 7:8) to describe the pollution of the flesh of a peace offering that is eaten on the third day after the sacrifice. Similarly, the Septuagint of Jeremiah 39:34 describes the idolatries of Judah as *miasmata* in the house of Yahweh. Far from being a clean and holy people, Peter is describing Judaism as a polluted and polluting world—whitewashed tombs that appear harmless but spread contagion of death. *Phthora* connotes physical corruption and again is an ironic description of Jews who believed that through keeping Torah they were avoiding contamination of decay. The references to dog's vomit and pig's mire reinforce this theme of the pollution of Judaism (2 Pet. 2:22; cf. Prov. 26:11), particularly since dogs and pigs were peculiarly unclean in the eyes of first-century Jews. Far from holding to the "holy commandment" by reverting to Judaism, they are turning from it (v. 21).

The narrative subtext of verses 18–22 is an exodus theme, and this again inverts Jewish self-understanding. Some have escaped from the overlordship of Pharaoh and of the world (v. 20) and are promising similar liberation to others (v. 19).[18] But the Judaizers and apostates to Judaism are like those Israelites who yearned to return to Egypt—return to bondage—and are in danger of suffering destruction along with Pharaoh and the Egyptians. They are people who have forgotten what Yahweh did to Egypt and have forgotten the purifying bath of the Exodus. They want to return to Egypt, and Peter wants to ensure that his readers will not be among those who return. Returning to Judaism is *not* returning to the people of the Exodus; it is a reversal of the Exodus, for Judaism is mystically Egypt.

Peter employs a great deal of ironic wordplay throughout the chapter.[19] He begins in verse 1 by noting that the false teachers introduce "destructive heresies." On the one hand, Peter is saying that heresies destroy the church, but on the other hand he is also saying that they are destructive for the false teachers themselves. By propagating destructive heresies, false teachers bring destruction on themselves. Destroyers of the church will be destroyed (1 Cor. 3:17). Structurally, the false teachers are contrasted with the

[18] The idea of liberation through law was common currency among Greeks of the first century. Michael Green writes, "Rival pagan schoolmen asserted that you escaped from the toils of corruption (*phthora*) by becoming participants in the divine nature either by means of *nomos* ('lawkeeping') or *phusis* ('nature')" (*2 Peter, Jude*, 73). Jews and Hellenized Jews offered the same promise through Torah.

[19] Bauckham, *Jude, 2 Peter*, is especially sensitive to the nuances of the Greek punning.

apostles that delivered the message of Jesus' power and coming. When we get to chapter 3, we will see that the teaching of the false teachers and the teaching of the apostles are polar opposites, just as Jeremiah's and the false prophets' teachings were. This contrast is already shown by the chiastic ordering of 2 Peter 1:16–2:3:

A. The apostles do not follow sophisticated myths.
  B. Prophecy comes from God.
  B'. But there have been false prophets.
A'. The false prophets teach false words.[20]

According to Peter, the destroyers will be destroyed "swiftly" (2:1; Greek: *tachine*). Moo concedes that "Peter may mean that the eschatological judgment will soon take place," but concludes instead that "rather than predicting the time of the judgment, 'swift' probably indicates its certainty."[21] This explanation fails mainly because the *time* of the judgment is precisely the issue throughout 2 Peter (cf. 3:4, and below). More than that, the word *tachine* cannot bear the meaning Moo wants to give it. Within the New Testament, the word is used only in 2 Peter but a related adverb, *tacheos*, is used with some frequency, and normally means "soon, without delay, quickly." A sampling will illustrate the point:

And the slave came back and reported to his master. Then the head of the household became angry and said to his slave, "Go at once [*tacheos*] into the streets and lanes of the city and bring in here the poor and crippled and blind and lame." (Lk. 14:21)

And he said, "A hundred measures of oil." And he said to him, "Take your bill, and sit down quickly [*tacheos*] and write fifty. (Lk. 16:6)

[20] Ibid., 238.
[21] Moo, *2 Peter, Jude*, 93.

The Jews then who were with her in the house, and consoling
her, when they saw that Mary rose up quickly [*tacheos*] and went
out, followed her. (Jn. 11:31)

I am amazed that you are so quickly [*tacheos*] deserting Him
who called you by the grace of Christ, for a different gospel.
(Gal. 1:6)

I trust in the Lord that I myself also shall be coming shortly
[*tacheos*]. (Phil. 2:24)

Do not lay hands on anyone hastily [*tacheos*] and thus share the
sins of others. (1 Tim. 5:22)

The adjective form (*tachine*) is used in 2 Peter 1:14 of Peter's "imminent" departure, and he surely intends to connect his "imminent" putting off of his tabernacle with the imminent destruction
of the false teachers. He will put off his tent, while the tent of the
false teachers will be torn to shreds like Shiloh.

Peter reinforces the imminence of the threat in 2:3 by personi-
fying judgment (it is "not idle") and destruction ("not asleep"). By
saying this, he is drawing on a thread of Old Testament prayer
that calls on God to "awake" in order to defend His people, destroy His enemies, and vindicate Himself and Israel:[22]

Arouse Thyself, why dost Thou sleep, O Yahweh? Awake, do not
reject us forever. Why dost Thou hide Thy face, and forget our
affliction and our oppression? (Ps. 44:23–24)

Recall the setting of the first-century church, and particularly of
Peter's readers, who have fled from Jerusalem because of persecution: Christian martyrs have spilled their blood in Jerusalem and

---

[22] See Bauckham, *Jude, 2 Peter,* 247–248.

elsewhere, beginning with Stephen, and for decades those who have been dispersed have been praying this Psalm. Peter is saying that these prayers will be answered, and that right soon. The plaintive "how long?" from the saints under the altar (Rev. 6:10) has been heard, and Peter assures his readers that the delay will not last forever (Rev. 10:6). In fact, the delay is nearly over.

Peter's description of the "swift" and "awakened" judgment of the false teachers shows that the judgment is a first-century event, not an event of the distant future. Indeed, no other interpretation makes sense. Destruction of false teachers is central to the coming destruction of the world (2:3; 3:7), which Peter has called the "day" and the "power and coming of Jesus." And he says that the destruction of ungodly men like the false teachers is "near," as near as Peter's own death, so near that the judgment is already at work ("not idle"). Thus the "coming" must also be imminent; the judgment of the world is already "awake" and ready to rumble. Surely Peter cannot be distinguishing between the time of the destruction of false teachers and the time of destruction of the present heavens and earth. If that were the case, the false teachers' mockery of Jesus' promise would be justified; in that case, the mockers would be exactly right to question the "promise of His coming" (3:4). Even if the false teachers were destroyed, they would eventually be proven right. Indefinite delay of the Parousia would be a feeble response to false teachers who are predicting that the Parousia will be delayed indefinitely! And God's judgments are not feeble.

Knock-Down Argument #3:

Peter says explicitly that the destruction of false teachers is coming "soon." Their destruction is the same event as the destruction of the present heavens and earth, the "day of judgment and destruction of ungodly men" (3:7). If the destruction of false teachers was near when Peter wrote, so also was the

> *destruction of the heavens and earth and the com-*
> *ing of a new heavens and earth.*

He's against the ropes. Next chapter, I'll deliver the final blows.

"THE JUDGE OF ALL EARTH DOES RIGHT": 2:4–22

At the center of Peter's letter, as I have already indicated, Peter tells a series of Old Testament stories to assure beleaguered Christians that God will judge the ungodly and that He will also rescue the righteous. These verses are central to Peter's concern, but less central to my own intentions in this commentary. Still, there are a number of intriguing puzzles in these verses, which are worth examining briefly. Again, a preterist interpretation of 2 Peter does not depend on any of the conclusions about this section of the letter, though applying a preterist framework to this section raises some stimulating questions of redemptive history.

First, a structural question must be addressed. Does Peter summarize two Old Testament incidents or three? It seems most natural as three separate incidents: (1) the angels cast into hell; (2) the ancient world destroyed and Noah preserved; and (3) Sodom and Gomorrah destroyed and Lot preserved. Alternatively, it could be that the "angels cast into hell" and the "ancient world" that was destroyed are just different versions of the same series of events recorded in Genesis 6–9. The repetition of "if he did not spare" in 2 Peter 2:4–5 supports the view that the imprisonment of the angels and the destruction of the "ancient world" are distinct incidents. If there are three, however, then they do not *all* make Peter's point. In verse 9, Peter draws the inference that the Lord knows how to rescue the godly and to keep the unrighteous under punishment, but the example of the angels does not show the Lord rescuing anybody. Thus the stories do not justify Peter's conclusion.

The *inclusio* in verses 4 and 9 helps to address this problem. Verse 4 speaks of angels "cast into hell and committed in pits of darkness reserved for judgment," while verse 9 states that the Lord will "keep the unrighteous under punishment for the day of judgment." Within this *inclusio*, Peter addresses a second issue—the Lord's rescue of the righteous in the day of wrath. Verse 9 as a whole thus draws two points from the preceding stories: (1) the Lord knows how to rescue the godly, and (2) he knows how to keep the wicked under confinement for the day of judgment. The second refers back to verse 4, while the first draws a conclusion from the examples of Noah and Lot. Verses 4–9 may thus be outlined as follows:

A. God holds the wicked under punishment for a day of judgment, angels as example (v. 4)
    B. God rescues the godly, Noah and Lot as examples (v. 5–8)
    B.' Summary: Lord knows how to rescue the godly (v. 9a)
A.' Summary: the Lord knows how to judge the wicked (v. 9b)

Peter cites three separate incidents—the angels, the flood, and Lot—and draws two distinct conclusions from these events.

ANGELS WHO SINNED

What are we to make of the "angels" of verse 4? The Old Testament background is the fall of the "sons of God" in Genesis 6. Contrary to many interpreters through the centuries, I do not believe that Genesis 6 reports that angels were picking up women in the ancient equivalent of singles' bars. Rather, it describes the fall of the Sethites, the faithful line descending from Adam's third son. In context, the question raised by Genesis 6:5 is, What happened to the faithful? And the answer is that the sons of God married the daughters of men and, like Solomon centuries later, were led astray. Moreover, the phrase "sons of God" connects back to the beginning of Genesis 5, where we are told that Adam was made in the likeness of God and Adam had a son in his own likeness, according to his own image. Since Adam was in the likeness of God, his son was also in the likeness of God. Seth, like Adam, is a "son of

God." When the phrase "sons of God" appears in Genesis 6:2, it has been prepared by 5:1–3. So Peter is not talking about the fall of spiritual beings but about the fall of the Sethites. It may seem odd to describe the Sethites as "angels," but in both Greek and Hebrew the word "angel" means "messenger," and the word is applied to both human and angelic messengers. Among the ancestors of the Sethites of the pre-flood generation was Enoch, identified as a prophet (Jude 14–15).

Like Satan in Revelation 20, these angels are being held under guard for a great day of judgment, at which time they will be cast out to their final and complete destruction. If we harmonize Revelation 20 and 2 Peter 3, we have this interesting repeated sequence from 'imprisonment' to future 'judgment':

Angels fall and are held for judgment
    Judgment comes on the world in the flood
Sodomites kept under punishment for day of judgment
    Judgment comes on Sodom
Present heavens and earth "kept" for day of judgment
    Judgment like Sodom (harlot, beast, false prophet judged)
Satan bound for one thousand years
    Final judgment of Satan and death

Yet Peter teaches more than a parallel between these incidents. This and other passages of the New Testament suggest that the Sethites who fell in the period before the flood were treated differently from other sinners; they have some unique role in the history of the world. In his first letter, Peter writes that the spirits who sinned in the days of Noah were committed to *tartarus*, held by chains or in pits of darkness until the time of judgment (1 Pet. 3:19–20), and proclamation was made to them after Jesus was "made alive in the Spirit."[23] Jude tells the story of angels who did

---

[23] See the superb treatment of this passage in Elliott, *1 Peter*, 637–710.

not keep their own *arche* but abandoned their proper abode (*oiketerion*). They were given an *arche*, a rule, a sphere of dominion, set up on the high places of the earth, but they did not guard their garden and are therefore kept for the "judgment of the great day." For Jude, this judgment day had not occurred, since he writes that the angels *are* still being kept *until* the day of judgment.

What day is that? The final judgment at the end of all history? Perhaps, but this is not how Peter talks about judgment day in either epistle, and it is unlikely that this is Jude's point either. In the context of 2 Peter, the judgment for which the "angels" are reserved is the same as the judgment that Peter discusses throughout the letter. He has spoken of the judgment that is not idle or asleep (2 Pet. 2:3), and in chapter 3 mentions the "day of judgment" (3:7) and the "day of God" (3:12). Within the preterist framework, we conclude that the angels who sinned were judged in the first-century judgment on the Old Covenant. Perhaps this is why 1 Peter 4:7 says that Jesus is "ready to judge the living and the dead." The fall of Jerusalem was a judgment not only of apostate Judaism, but on the pre-flood generation as well. All the blood from Abel on were charged to that generation.

Although some points yet remain unclear, several conclusions may still be drawn. First, Peter draws a parallel between the Lord's treatment of the "angels" in 2 Peter 2:4 and the plans for the "present heavens and earth" in 3:7. In both cases, something is being "kept" for a later time (the angels "kept" for the day of judgment and the present heavens and earth "kept" for fire). Sentence has been pronounced and will be executed, but there is a period of confinement, of "keeping," before final execution. So it is appropriate for Peter to cite the example of the angels in describing the future of false prophets. Like the former, the latter are being "kept" for later judgment. Like the angels who sinned, the false teachers are going to end up "in black darkness."

Second, this means that the "day of God" that Peter is talking

about is not merely the end of the Mosaic order, or the order of the
world organized around Israel, or the world-order of the post-exilic period. Rather, the "day of God" will bring an end to the "heavens and earth" that existed from the time of the flood, and will also
put the finishing touches on the judgment of those who sinned *before*
the flood. The post-flood world, with all its variations, is treated as
a single "world" or "heavens and earth." When the day of God
comes, it will bring the post-flood world to an end and inaugurate
a new heavens and earth through a judgment of fire.

Third, it might seem odd to think that the events in Jerusalem
would have something to do with judgment on the prelapsarian
wicked, but the New Testament is clear that the work of Christ's
first coming—His death, resurrection, and ascension—affected
the dead as well as the living. Hebrews 11 lists all these Old Testament saints and ends by saying that they died without receiving
what was promised because they were going to receive "something
better" along with "us" Christians (v. 40). This is consistent with the
overall theology of Hebrews. Jesus is the forerunner who enters
the Most Holy Place before any others, before the Old Testament
saints. It seems plausible that Jesus' final act of establishing the New
Creation, His judgment on Jerusalem, would have some similar
effects on the wicked dead. They are confined in darkness, but when
Jesus brings the present heavens and earth to an end, they will be
judged too. Not only the martyrs of Judaism, but all martyrs are
being avenged in the first century: all the blood from righteous
Abel onward is charged to "this generation" (Mt. 23:34–36).
Clearly the end of the present heavens and earth is not merely an
event in Middle Eastern history, but an event of global significance.

NOAH AND RIGHTEOUS LOT
Peter's two other Old Testament references to judgment are more
straightforward. The mention of Noah's flood and the destruction
of Sodom anticipates the judgments by water and fire in chapter 3.

Moreover, there are intriguing parallels between Noah and Lot which are already apparent in Genesis. Both men escape from a world that is being destroyed, both escape with family members (though Lot, unlike Noah, loses his wife), both drink wine, and both are plotted against by their children (Ham sees Noah naked in his tent and plots to seize the robe, while Lot's daughters make him drunk and then sleep with him). Lot's daughters produce Moab and Ammon, while the incident with Ham ends with the curse on Canaan and the future Canaanites.

These parallels underscore Peter's claim that Lot was a righteous man, which he is called three times in two verses (2:7–8). To many readers, Genesis suggests otherwise, apparently depicting Lot as a weak, vacillating backslider. To be sure, Lot makes some foolish decisions, particularly in settling near Sodom, but Genesis also brings out extensive similarities not only between Lot and righteous Noah, but between Lot and righteous Abraham. Both are visited by the angels and both respond by offering hospitality and preparing a meal.[24] Lot shows his righteousness by contrast.

The main point, of course, is that the readers of Peter's letter find themselves in a situation similar to Noah and Lot. They are surrounded by wicked people, and especially by false teachers. This is their "trial" (v. 9), and the Lord will rescue them just as he rescued Noah and Lot, by destroying their enemies and giving them a way of escape. Peter wants his readers to seek safety in the new ark that is currently under construction, the Christian church, and in flight from the Sodomite city that is about to be destroyed.

SENSUALITY AND REBELLION
Beginning in 2:10, Peter focuses attention on the character of the false teachers. He does not treat the *content* of their teaching until

---

[24] This is the background to later condemnations of Sodom and Gomorrah by the prophets, who condemn the cities because they did not show proper hospitality, but instead sexually assaulted the angelic visitors (Ezek. 16:49).

chapter 3, but instead attacks their evil *conduct*. His summary statement of 2:10 summarizes the two main charges: they "indulge the flesh" and "despise authority." As I have suggested above, these are highly provocative descriptions of Christian Jews who have apostatized, but it is also likely that Peter's opponents were actually arrogant and sexually promiscuous. Peter takes these two main charges in reverse order in verses 10–16, and we should look at his condemnatory expositions of the charges in a bit more detail.

First, Peter charges the false teachers with despising authority. The false teachers' opposition to authority is illustrated by their boldness in reviling or blaspheming "glories," even though angels who are greater in power and might do not revile (cf. Jude 8–9). Calvin says the glories are magistrates and emperors, while others have suggested that the word refers to church authorities. Most recent commentators argue that the glories are some kind of angelic being (whether good angels or demons is debated). It seems unlikely that evil angels would be described as "glories," and it would also be odd to condemn anyone for *blaspheming* evil angels or Satan. Yet verse 11 seems to be describing good angels who refuse to revile the "glories," thus implying that the good angels might have a *right* to revile the glories.

Alternatively the "glories" might be taken as the glorious ones (the saints of the Old Covenant) or as the glories of the Old Covenant order such as the temple, the priesthood, the covenants, and all the things that made Israel glorious. False teachers revile glories of the Old Covenant. This is the charge falsely made against Jesus, Stephen, and Paul, but, in an ironic reversal, Peter says it is false Judaizing teachers who blaspheme against the glories.[25] Peter's point is similar to Paul's in Galatians 4: you who appeal to the law,

---

[25] There might also be a reference to angelic beings: "Glories" might refer to those angels whom the New Testament says were mediators of the law (Acts 7:53; Gal. 3:19).

do you actually read it? At the very moment when the Judaizers are claiming to be the upholders of Torah, they are denying Torah. On this view, the "angels" of verse 11 are not spiritual beings, but messengers or heralds. "Angel" is used consistently throughout this chapter to refer to righteous human beings, especially messengers of the covenant. In verse 4 it refers to the Sethite prophets, and here it refers to messengers of the New Covenant, those who were accused of blaspheming the glories but did not. These messengers of the New Covenant did not bring before the Lord a blasphemous judgment against the glories of the Old Covenant, but honored the fathers far more than those who persecuted the prophets.

According to verse 12, the false teachers are like unreasoning animals that are good only for being hunted down. This is a continuation of Peter's charge that they despise authority. They are not like domestic animals that submit to the voice of a master but like wild animals who are ruled purely by instinct. Fittingly, their end is going to be like that of unreasoning animals, as they are chased down, captured, and destroyed (by Roman legions). They will receive fit payment for their labor—evil consequences as wages for doing evil.

Second, Peter charges the false teachers with sensuality. Sensuality and adultery are, as noted above, frequent images of false worship and idolatry in the Bible. Descriptions of this kind of spiritual adultery can get realistically graphic (Ezekiel 16 and 23, for example). Yet idolatry and spiritual adultery are often manifested in literal sexual immorality and adultery, and Peter's description seems to include this charge as well. In 2 Peter, the false teachers are lovers of pleasure who "revel in the day" (2:13). Peter's use of "day" has a fulness here, implying that the false teachers are reveling with the day approaching, acting as if the day is not coming. Their lives are consistent with their confidence that everything will continue as it always has. Peter also describes them as "stains" and "blemishes," both sacrificial terms that indicate that the false teachers defile the body of Christ, are themselves disqualified as priests, and make the church an unacceptable sacrifice (cf. 3:14 by contrast). If the church offers herself to God when she is full of such stains and blemishes, he will spew her out of His mouth. The false teachers also revel in their "deceptions" as they "feast together" with the readers. Peter puns on *agape*, saying that the false teachers revel not in their *agapais* (love feasts) but in their *apatais* (deceptions). Their feasting is not an expression of Christlike love, but is deceptive. Their "love feasts" are "deceptions."

False teachers are not satisfied to revel in their own deceptions; they lure, entice, and bait others. The metaphor is from hunting or fishing; the false teachers, like the apostles, are fishers of men, but they fish in order to destroy not to save. Ironically, the false teachers are setting bait for others, but they are themselves "unreasoning creatures" who are destined to be trapped. Also ironically, Peter contrasts the "unstable souls" who are influenced by false teachers with the disciplined greed of the false teachers. The Greek word for "trained" is the word behind "gymnasium" and suggests disciplined practice (v. 14). Accomplished gymnasts not in godliness but greed, their practice and training make them effective in seducing and destroying flabby souls.

Two threads of Peter's denunciation lead to the example of Balaam. On the surface, the false teachers are like Balaam in that they are greedy, another sign of their lustfulness and slavery to evil desire. Balaam agreed to curse Israel for money, and these false teachers stain the church because they find the occupation lucrative. More subtly, Balaam was also responsible for leading the people of Israel into idolatry and sexual immorality. In Numbers 25, at Peor, the Israelites became like the "angels who sinned," abandoning their place and going after the daughters of Midian. In Numbers 31:16, we learn that the Midianite women seduced the Israelites through the counsel of Balaam. Since Balak's direct assault on Israel did not work, Balaam led Israel astray by seduction to idolatry and fornication. The dragon in Revelation 12 uses similar tactics. When his direct assault on the child and woman fails, he goes to plan B, spewing poisonous water of heresy from his mouth, seducing the angels with the daughters of men. Peter says that the false teachers do the same—they are sons of Balaam.

There are several puns in 2 Peter 2:15–16. In most manuscripts, Balaam is called the son of "Bosor," though in the Old Testament he is called the "son of Beor." This is probably a Greek transliteration of *basar*, "flesh."[26] Balaam, the son of flesh, loves the wages of unrighteousness, but the wages of doing wrong is to suffer wrong (v. 13). Balaam's wages for his unrighteousness was to be killed with the Midianites (Num. 31:8): if you love the wages of unrighteousness, you will end up receiving the wages of unrighteousness. There is also a pun on "transgression" and "madness." Balaam is rebuked for his *paranomia* (transgression) by the donkey who restrained his *paraphronia* (madness).[27] Of course, Peter wants us to see the irony of a great seer being rebuked by a donkey. False teachers are unreasoning animals; in fact, like Balaam, they are worse, since even a donkey knows more than they do.

False teachers are dangerous, and ultimately they are futile, empty, and vain. They produce no life or fruit (v. 17). A teacher is supposed to be a spring of living water, watering the garden of the church, offering thirst-quenching water. But these teachers are dry springs and mists, which offer no heavenly rain or ground water. Like the angels, they are destined for darkness because they have ignored the lamp shining in the darkness that alone would lead them to the day. Instead of passing mists, they will someday be overshadowed with impenetrable darkness.

In verses 19–22, Peter returns to the accusation of apostasy with which he began in verse 1, and it is clear this apostasy has actually

---

[26] Bauckham, *Jude, 2 Peter,* 267.
[27] Ibid., 269.

happened. These false teachers, Peter claims, were bought by the Master, redeemed and incorporated into Christ and His kingdom, but have now turned against Christ and returned to their earlier way of life. Both "master" and "bought" conjure the image of manumission. Once the teachers were delivered from slavery, and once they actually escaped the defilements of the world. They were among those who were led from Egypt. Now, however, they have returned to slavery, overcome again by the defilements of the world, enslaved to a new master which is really their old master. This is one of the most explicit statements in the New Testament that apostasy is possible and that the apostate is in worse condition than the unbeliever. "It would have been better" if they had never known the truth, for now they have become like unclean animals, dogs and pigs. Like Judas, it would have been better if they had never been born.

4
THREE WORLDS

By this point, I hope I have made a plausible case that Peter's entire letter is about a set of prophecies that Peter expected to be fulfilled during his readers' lifetimes. My knock-down arguments have accumulated, and there are still two more to come. From the beginning, Peter has been dealing with the prophecy of Jesus that "there are some standing here who will not taste death until you see the Son of Man coming in His kingdom." 2 Peter 3 must be consistent with the overall thrust of the letter.

Though it does not (quite) qualify as a knock-down argument, the chiastic structure of the letter shows that Peter returns in 3:1–13 to a discussion of the same prophecy mentioned in the second half of chapter 1 (1:12–21). Several details are common to these two sections. First, several times in 1:12–15 Peter states his intention is to remind his readers, and 3:1–2 returns to this theme with another fragrant cluster of "remembrance" terms. Second, Peter returns explicitly to prophecies of the "coming" of Jesus. First mentioned in 1:16, where Peter defended his teaching by appeal to two witnesses, this theme comes up again in 3:4, where Peter addresses mockers who doubt the "promise of his coming." Finally, the terminology of the "day" is found in both sections (as it is also found in chapter 2). 1:19 speaks of the "dawning of the day," and 3:10, 12 of

the "day of the Lord" and the "day of God," while verse 7 tells about
the "day of judgment and destruction of ungodly men." If Peter has
a specific prophecy in mind in 1:16–19—the prophecy of Jesus that
He would come in power with His angels before the generation of
the apostles has passed—and if 3:1–13 is structurally parallel to
1:16–19, using some of the same terminology and addressing some
of the same concerns, then the two passages must be, as they say,
mutually interpreting. If 1:16–19 is concerned with the prophecy
of Jesus' coming within the first century, this must be the same
prophecy being discussed in 3:1–13.

Even before the detailed examination of chapter 3, then, we have
good reason to suspect that the chapter will be about the imminent
judgment on the Old Creation. These suspicions, I argue below, are
fully justified.

"THE DAY": 3:1–13

As preterist interpreters have pointed out, there are indications
within chapter 3 that Peter is talking about a "day of judgment" that
would occur within the first century. Peter is concerned with
mockers who arise in the church in the "last days," and this and similar phrases refer throughout the New Testament to the apostolic
era, not some future period of history:

> Now these things happened to them as a type, and were written
> for our instruction, on whom the ends of the ages have come.
> (1 Cor. 10:11)

> God, after He spoke long ago to the fathers in the prophets in
> many portions and in many ways, in these last days has spoke to
> us in His Son. (Heb. 1:1–2)

> For [Christ] was foreknown before the foundation of the
> world, but has appeared in these last times for the sake of you.
> (1 Pet. 1:20)

Peter warns that mockers will come in the first century (2 Pet. 3:3), and this implies that their "destruction" must also take place within that period. As noted above in chapter 2, the mockers are the same as the false teachers of 2 Peter 2; the false teachers are the "ungodly men" of 3:7 and the "unprincipled men" of 3:17.[1] Thus the "day of God" (3:12) is the "day" for the destruction of the false teachers (3:7). If the mockers have already appeared in the first century, and their destruction is predicted, that destruction must also take place in the first century.[2] It would hardly be worthwhile for God to destroy the false teachers long after they have died. Since the destruction of the ungodly teachers is part and parcel of the end of the heavens and earth, then the destruction of heaven and earth must also be expected in the first century.

The phrase "last days" also has a broader reference in some passages, designating not only the apostolic period but the whole period from the exile through the apostolic period, the whole period of the "seventy weeks" of Daniel 9. About Nebuchadnezzar's vision of the statue, Daniel says that God "has made known to King Nebuchadnezzar what will take place in the end of the days" (Dan. 2:28), and he goes on to explain that the vision begins with Nebuchadnezzar himself (2:38). Similarly, a vision of the wars that followed Alexander's campaigns (Dan. 11) gives "understanding of what will happen to your people in the end of the days" (Dan. 10:14). These uses in Daniel are rooted in the prophecies of Moses at the end of Deuteronomy:

---

[1] 2 Pet. 3:17 uses the same word ("unprincipled") as 2:7, which draws an analogy between the false teachers and Sodomites.

[2] Hillyer gives a good description of the psychology of Peter's readers: "No doubt some of Peter's readers, galled by the pernicious workings of the false teachers, must often have asked how long God would allow the situation to persist. In his role as pastor, Peter reassures them. Divine deliverance may seem to be uncertain, or at least long in coming. But it will come, for God is in control all along" (*1 and 2 Peter, Jude*, 191). In Hillyer's futurist interpretation, however, it is difficult to see how Peter provides any sort of reassurance.

For I know that after my death you will act corruptly and turn
from the way which I have commanded you; and evil will befall
you in the latter days, for you will do that which is evil in the
sight of Yahweh, provoking Him to anger with the work of your
hands. (Deut. 31:29)

In Moses' and Daniel's scheme, the "former days" of Israel's history
include the Exodus and the period of the kingdom, while the "latter
days" are the period when Israel bowed before a series of imperial
world powers. For the apostles, however, the phrasing has a more
specific reference to the period at the end of the "latter days" or the
"times of the Gentiles." We might say that Peter is describing events
of the "latter days of the latter days."

From the perspective of Daniel, we can conclude that the end of
the "latter days" that Peter predicts means an end (at least) to an entire world-order in which Israel was subjected to Gentile protec-
tors and powers. Judgment on the "present heavens and earth" is not
only a judgment on Jerusalem but on the entire political economy
of the postexilic world. Revelation reveals this same point by depicting the fall of the beast, a composite of the four beasts of Daniel
7 (cf. Rev. 13:1–10), and the fall of the false prophet, who repre-
sents Jews in their cooperation with pagan imperialism.[3]

The specific content of the mockers' mockery decisively supports a preterist interpretation. This is a knock-down argument to
end all knock-down arguments. Seeing that the first generation of
believers (the "fathers," 3:4; see below) are passing on with no sign
that the "power and coming" of Jesus is imminent, the mockers ask,
"Where is the promise of His coming?" (3:4). They do not believe
that the Parousia is being delayed but are questioning whether or
not it will ever occur. Now these doubts would arise *only* if they
had reason to expect the Parousia to happen soon. And they are a
threat to Peter's readers, able to sway and perhaps persuade some

---

[3] For more, see Jordan, *A Brief Reader's Guide to Revelation*.

of them, *only* because they seem to have a point. Had Jesus said, "I am coming, but I won't say when," the subsequent passage of time would not undermine the prophecy at all. Suppose, however, Jesus said something like "Some who are standing here will not taste death until they see the Son of Man coming in His kingdom" or "Before this generation passes, all these things shall be fulfilled." If He said that, then the passing of the first generation would indeed raise doubts about His promise. But wherever would the mockers have gotten the idea that Jesus was coming before the "fathers" died? Why, lo and behold, Jesus said *exactly* that.

The whole debate presupposes that Jesus promised to come *soon*. Without that premise, neither the mockers' mockery nor Peter's letter makes any sense. Peter and his opponents differ on the crucial question of the promise's reliability, but they agree on its content. Bauckham recognizes the force of this point:

> [T]he critical point for the nonfulfillment of the promise of the Parousia came at the time when it could be said that the generation of the apostles had died. The objection of the scoffers was not just that a long time had passed since the promise was given, but that the promise itself had set a time-limit within which it would be fulfilled and this time-limit had passed.[4]

Yet Bauckham rejects this interpretation. First, he argues that if the scoffers were claiming that the terminus had passed, "their objection ought to be, not that nothing has happened since the fathers died, but that nothing happened before they died." It is hard to see the force of this objection. Bauckham himself translates verse 4 this way: "the fathers have died and *still* nothing happens" (his italics). One can easily take this to mean that everyone expected something to happen *before* the fathers died: "We expected Jesus to come prior to the death of the apostles, but now we are past that time and nothing has happened even yet." Bauckham's translation actually

---

[4] Bauckham, *Jude, 2 Peter,* 291–292.

makes *better* sense if the scoffers expected something to happen before the death of the fathers.

Second, he claims that "2 Peter does not *answer* the objection that a specific time-limit has passed" but instead simply "reproduces the answers to the problem of eschatological delay which he found in his Jewish apocalyptic source." But as Bauckham himself recognizes, Peter *does* answer the question of delay by stating that (1) the prophetic word (of Jesus) has reserved the present heavens and earth for fire, and therefore it will be burned, and that (2) God has patiently and graciously extended the time for "all to come to repentance" (3:9). Neither of these responses means that Peter raises "the issue of eschatological delay above the level of calculating dates." To do so would be against the grain of biblical prophecy, which is very much concerned with calculating dates. Peter is still confident that Jesus will do what He said He would do, namely, come within "this generation."

Knock-Down Argument #4:

Peter responds to mockers who doubt the promise of Jesus' coming because time has passed without any sign of the Parousia. If there were no time limit on the original prophecy, then the mockers would have no grounds for their mockery and no way to attract converts to their skeptical views. Therefore, the original prophecy must have included a time limit, a **terminus ad quem,** *and that time limit must have been the lifetime of the apostles.*

He's against the ropes and in a corner. One more should do it.

MOCKERS
As in chapter 2, Peter draws parallels between his opponents and the false prophets of the Old Testament, particularly the preexilic

prophets in Jeremiah's time, who were also skeptical about predictions of judgment. In Jeremiah 17:15, Jeremiah's opponents ask, "Where is the word of the Lord? Let it come now."[5] The parallel is quite exact. Old Testament prophets assured the faithful they would be vindicated while the faithless would be punished, but the mocking false prophets say, "If God is on your side, where is He? You've suffered at the hands of persecutors, and you expect God to rescue you. Where is this vindication that you predicted?"

The question that Peter attributes to the mockers is phrased like the questions of the scoffers and mockers of the Psalms, who taunt the suffering psalmist: "Why isn't God intervening to rescue you, if the Lord delights in you?" (42:3, 10). In some passages the mockers raise the same question to Israel:

> Help us, O God of our salvation, for the glory of Thy name; and deliver us, and forgive our sins, for Thy name's sake. Why should the nations say, "Where is their God?" Let there be known among the nations in our sight, vengeance for the blood of Thy servants, which has been shed. . . . And return to our neighbors sevenfold into their bosom the reproach with which they have reproached Thee, O Yahweh. (Ps. 79:9–12)

> Why should the nations say, "Where, now, is their God?" (Ps. 115:2)

> Let the priests . . . say, "Spare Thy people, O Yahweh, and do not make Thine inheritance a reproach, a byword among the nations. Why should they among the peoples say, Where is their God?" (Joel 2:17)

Peter thus casts the false teachers in the role of Gentile nations who taunt Israel, in the place of the persecutors who taunt the faithful,

---

[5] In Malachi 2:17 we see warnings from the prophet that Israel has wearied God by doing evil and then saying, "Where is the God of justice?"

and in the place of false prophets. Jewish false teachers, who claim to be Jews but are not, have become "Gentiles," while the Christians are the true Jews.[6]

Peter's characterization of his opponents highlights the importance of Jesus' Parousia in first-century Christianity. We tend to think of a diversity of millennial views as tolerable, perhaps even healthy, for the Christian church. Outside super-strict Dispensationalist circles, no one is counted a heretic or apostate because he believes in a post-tribulation-pre-Raphaelite-pre-millennial full rapture instead of a pre-tribulation-post-modern-premillennial partial rapture. Peter is not nearly so tolerant. Those who mock the promise of Jesus' coming, of His *imminent* coming, are false teachers, men who have "denied the Master who bought them," dogs and pigs who return to their previous *miasma*.

The reason Peter takes this with such high seriousness is not difficult to fathom, though it has been forgotten or ignored for centuries. As N. T. Wright has recently argued, Jesus' prediction of a coming destruction of the city and temple, developed at length in the Olivet Discourse, was a test case of His claims to be a true prophet and Messiah. A true prophet is one whose predictions come to pass. Jeremiah was a true prophet because he predicted the destruction of Jerusalem and it happened; the false prophets of his day were false prophets because they predicted peace that never came. If Jesus predicted the fall of Jerusalem and predicted that it would happen within a generation—which He did—then He can be considered a true prophet *only* if it came to pass—which it did.[7] To put

---

[6] Mockery is also a theme of wisdom literature, found in the Psalms and Proverbs, where the "mocker" or scoffer is one who despises all wisdom and instruction. Righteous men do not "sit in the seat of the scoffers" (Ps. 1:1), and wisdom calls to scoffers to turn from their scoffing (Prov. 1:22). Denying the promise of the Parousia brands Peter's opponents as fools and scoffers, like dogs who return to their vomit (Prov. 26:11).

[7] Wright, *Jesus and the Victory of God*, especially chapter 8.

it bluntly, if Jesus did not come to vindicate, He is not the Messiah. If He did not come to vindicate Himself and His bride *within the time He set*, He is not the Messiah. But He did, and He is.

I am not prepared to say that non-preterists are apostates, but I hope for the day when Jesus' prophecies will be so universally understood that they will be considered so; or, failing that, for the day when non-preterists will seem as exotic a species as postmillennialists seem today.

THE FATHERS HAVE FALLEN ASLEEP

The mockers' skepticism about the Parousia is based on the fact that although the "fathers" have fallen asleep, things continue on as they have since creation. Normally, "fathers" in the New Testament refers to the Old Testament patriarchs and forefathers, who are considered the fathers of the Christian church (cf. 1 Cor. 10:1; Heb. 1:1; 3:9; 8:9). If the mockers are skeptical because the Parousia did not come before Old Testament saints died, it is difficult to see the point. If this were their objection, their skepticism would be directed toward prophecy in general, or it would imply that they expected the promises of the Parousia to be fulfilled within the lifetime of the Old Testament fathers, an odd view indeed. Neither is in dispute in Peter's letter.

What *is* in dispute is Jesus' promise that He would come before the end of the apostolic generation, while "some who are standing here" are still alive.[8] Given this, "fathers" must refer to the "fathers" or "patriarchs" of the Christian church. This use of the term "fathers" is, so far as I have found, unique in the New Testament, but it is a perfectly natural extension of several fixed threads of New Testament usage. Paul, for starters, commonly speaks of his disciples,

---

[8] Again, the structural considerations reviewed above shed valuable light on Peter's point. The Parousia in 3:4 parallels the reference to the Parousia in 1:16, and therefore the promise in dispute in 3:4 is specifically Jesus' promise to come in glory before the end of the apostolic generation.

Timothy especially, as "children" and "sons," implying that he is in a paternal relationship with them:

> I do not write these things to shame you, but to admonish you as my beloved children. (1 Cor. 4:14)

> Now in a like exchange—I speak as to children—open wide to us also. (2 Cor. 6:13)

> We were exhorting and encouraging and imploring each one of you as a father would his own children. (1 Thes. 2:11)

> Paul, an apostle of Christ Jesus according to the commandment of God our Savior, and of Christ Jesus, who is our hope, to Timothy, my true child in faith. (1 Tim. 1:1–2)

> Paul, an apostle of Christ Jesus by the will of God . . . to Timothy my beloved son. . . . [M]y son, be strong in the grace that is in Christ Jesus. (2 Tim. 1:1–2; 2:1)

The example of Timothy is particularly useful, since Paul trained him to carry on the work of the apostolic church. Apostles and those directly associated with them thus formed a paternal generation while Timothy and others trained by the apostles were a filial generation. It would be natural, then, for someone of Timothy's generation to look back to the apostles as "fathers" in the faith. Moreover, Jesus deliberately chose twelve disciples in order to send the message that He was forming a new Israel, and it again would be quite natural that the following generation would look back to the apostles as "patriarchs" of the new Israel (just as we talk about "Church Fathers" of the post-apostolic period).[9]

[9] The transition from a paternal, apostolic generation to a filial, second generation accords with the Exodus typology so pervasive in the New Testament. Jesus underwent an exodus in Jerusalem (Lk. 9:31), and the apostles were the

This makes the mockers' argument very specific, pointed, and persuasive to some. Jesus had promised that His Parousia would occur before the first generation had passed ("there are some standing here," "this generation shall not pass until all these things are fulfilled"). But now the "fathers" are falling asleep. True, the fathers' generation has not completely passed since Peter himself is still alive, but fathers *are* falling asleep and no cataclysmic judgment is on the horizon. Almost all modern commentators agree that the "fathers" are the first generation of Christians. Yet few recognize the implication that the mockery of the scoffers *only* makes sense if they are contesting a promise that the Parousia would occur *before* the fathers had fallen asleep. If Jesus had said, "These things are going to be fulfilled in some uncertain time-frame," the passing of the fathers would be as irrelevant as the passing of the dodo. If, however, they are disputing a prophecy of the Parousia that had specific reference to the apostolic generation, then the mockery makes sense. Wherever did they get the idea that Jesus would return before the fathers died? Lo and behold, Jesus made exactly *that* promise.

Knock-Down Argument #5:

For the mockers, the passing of the "fathers," the apostles and their associates, casts doubt on the truth of Jesus' promise to come in power. This objection has weight only if Jesus had in fact promised to come before the "fathers" passed from the scene. Thus the prophecy in dispute in 2 Peter 3 promised a

---

"fathers" who escaped from Egypt with him. Now they are all in the wilderness, and the children who did not witness the Exodus have to be reminded of things they did not witness. Some of the "children" are getting restive, threatening to return to Egypt, or, to shift the typology slightly, the children are camped at Moab but reluctant to claim the land, since they are no longer certain that Jericho will fall.

> *"coming" within the apostolic generation. The*
> *prophecy Peter says will be fulfilled is a prophecy*
> *about Jesus' coming within the generation.* [10]

That, I should think, fairly ends the fight. I have a few scratches, but by my reckoning, it's a win by TKO, if not an outright KO.

WORLD THAT THEN WAS

Whatever Peter goes on to say has to be consistent with our findings to this point. If 2 Peter is at all coherent, his discussion of the end of a world and the beginning of another are part of a discussion about Jesus' promise to come within the generation of the apostles.

Peter does not directly respond to the statement about the passing of the fathers, although verses 8–9 may be considered an indirect response. Instead he considers the statement in the latter part of verse 4 to be crucial to the mockers' position and addresses that directly. The mockery assumes a uniformitarian view of history. Things move on as they always have and there are no catastrophic occurrences. This may not have been their overt theory of history, but their objections to Jesus' promise betrays their tacit assumption (hope?) that God does not intervene in history. Such skepticism is consistent with their mocking question, with its Old Testament echoes: "Where is the God of justice? The wicked prosper, life goes on, and God is nowhere to be found. Where is now the God of Israel?"

How is this consistent with my earlier identification of the false teachers as Jews (see previous chapter)? Jews, after all, should know better than anyone that world history is not uniformitarian, that it is punctuated by activity from outside, that Yahweh is a meddling God who pokes His arm and hand into time and toys with

---

[10] Admittedly this is a variation of the same punch I threw earlier, but old ways are the best ways.

nations and empires. This is a difficulty that I cannot resolve fully, but several points may be made toward a resolution. First, my distinction between the mockers' "overt" and "implicit" view of history is supported by the ironic tone of Peter's reminder of the creation and flood: "it escapes their notice that . . ." (v. 5). This introductory clause implies that Peter's opponents were in fact quite familiar with the creation and flood accounts, though they had not drawn the proper conclusions from those events. The sarcastic tone is similar to Paul's: "You who want to be under law, do you not listen to the law?" (Gal. 4:21).

Second, this same charge could be leveled at the false prophets in the days of Jeremiah, who were undoubtedly Jewish. Though they recognized that Yahweh was active in history, they believed that the temple and city of Jerusalem, at least, were impervious. Nations might rise and fall, but the house of Yahweh would stand forever, and as long as they took their stand there, no Nebuchadnezzar could touch them. Again, these false prophets would undoubtedly have confessed that Yahweh rules all things and intervenes frequently in history, but they did not believe that there could be a change of the magnitude that Jeremiah envisioned. Jewish and Judaizing opponents of the early church held very similar views: even *if* a New Covenant has come, that *cannot* mean that circumcision, food laws, and laws of cleanness are now irrelevant, and the coming of the Messiah *cannot* mean that "circumcision is nothing, nor uncircumcision" (Gal. 6:15).

A third, related point may also be made. It was common for Jews to believe that Torah was begotten along with the creation. Linking "Wisdom" and Torah, and reading this linkage into Proverbs 8, led Jews to conclude that Torah was the agent of the original creation, and that Torah was in fact the purpose for which God created the world. W. D. Davies summarizes this view under three headings:

1. The Torah, like Wisdom, came to be regarded as older than the world. Thus it is the first among the seven things which were created before the world. Again in *Sifre* on Deut. 11.10, Prov. 8.22 is taken to mean that the Law was created before everything. "The Law because it is more highly prized (literally, dearer) than everything, was created before everything. . . ."

2. Secondly, the Torah is brought into connection with creation: e.g., R. Akiba said: "Beloved are Israel to whom was given a precious instrument wherewith the world was created. . . ."

3. Thirdly, the world is claimed to be created for the sake of Torah. Thus R. Yudan said: "The world was created for the sake (literally: because of the merit) of the Torah." Moore also quotes a far earlier passage in this connection, the aphorism of Simeon the Just: "The stability of the world rests on three things, on the Law, on 'worship,' and on deeds of personal kindness."[11]

Believing that Torah was eternal and unchanging in a quite literal sense, they did not believe it could be modified in the radical way the apostles claimed. Yahweh might well act in history, but the Jews refused to let Him act like *that*.

Peter's response to the mockers is designed to address precisely this view. He is not responding to the notion that *no* historical changes can occur, which is too absurd to require refutation. He is responding to the claim that no historical changes can displace the "present heavens and earth" to make room for "a new heavens and earth." Whatever historical changes might be made, Torah, temple, and Israel's centrality will remain unchanged. Whatever historical changes occur, it cannot be said that they constitute the beginning of a new creation.

Peter's examples show, in fact, the Creator has made a habit of

[11] W.D. Davies, *Paul and Rabbinic Judaism: Some Rabbinic Elements in Pauline Theology* (Mifflintown: Sigler Press, 1998), 170–171. Adapting these claims to the gospel, Paul argues that Jesus takes the place of Torah; the apostolic emphasis on Jesus' fulfillment of the Law is both a hermeneutical and theological point.

forming new worlds from time to time. He first points out that the creation is completely a contingent product of God's word and working. Creation is not a self-sustaining, uniform continuum, and if it was brought into being by the word of God, it can be snuffed out by the word of God. Peter distinguishes between the creation of the heavens and the creation of the earth—the former is created "by the word of God," while the earth was "formed out of water and by water." This is consistent with the creation account. Both the high heavens (Gen. 1:1) and the firmament (1:6–7) were created directly by the word of God, while the earth (i.e., everything other than the heavens) took shape by a hydraulic process, as Yahweh God separated the waters above and below as well as the waters and land.[12] We shall return to this distinction below.

Importantly for Peter's purposes, this same word was the agent for the world's destruction (v. 6). The prepositional phrase "through which" is difficult because the relative pronoun is plural: "through which things." What is it referring to? The best sense is made if the plural pronoun refers to the word and water by which "the world that then was" was destroyed. There is thus a parallel between the way creation came into existence and the way the "world that then was" was brought to an end. Word and water both create and destroy. Verse 7 applies this to Peter's circumstances: if heaven and earth were made by the word and water and if the world was also destroyed by word and water, then if the word declares that the "present heavens and earth" are destined for judgment by fire, then it is going to happen.

Where has the word reserved the "present heavens and earth" for

---

[12] This suggests a connection with baptism. In his first letter, Peter already described baptism by referring to the typology of the flood (1 Pet. 3:18–22), and here he is talking about a creation emerging by God's power through the agency of water. It is not merely that the earth was formed "out of" water (*ek*); water was also the agent of creation (*dia*, "through"). Baptism, likewise, forms a new creation out of the dust and clay of a son of Adam.

fire? This is virtually impossible to answer unless we recognize that both John and Jesus, throughout their ministries, were telling parables and issuing prophecies about the imminent doom of Israel. Jesus is the eschatological prophet, the final prophet of the final doom for the Old Covenant people of God, and this doom is over and over spoken of as a fiery destruction:

> Do not suppose that you can say to yourselves, "We have Abraham for our father"; for I say to you that God is able from these stones to raise up children to Abraham. And the axe is already laid at the root of the trees; every tree therefore that does not bear good fruit is cut down and thrown into the fire. . . . He who is coming after me is mightier than I, and I am not fit to remove His sandals; He will baptize you with the Holy Spirit and fire. And His winnowing fork is in His hand, and He will thoroughly clear His threshing floor; and He will gather His wheat into the barn, but He will burn up the chaff with unquenchable fire. (Mt. 3:8–12)

> Just as the tares are gathered up and burned with fire, so shall it be at the end of the age. The Son of Man will send forth His angels, and they will gather out of His kingdom all stumbling blocks [like followers of Balaam], and those who commit lawlessness, and will cast them into the furnace of fire; in that place there shall be weeping and gnashing of teeth. (Mt. 13:40–42)

> Just as the lightning, when it flashes out of one part of the sky, shines to the other part of the sky, so will the Son of Man be in His day. . . . It was the same as happened in the days of Lot: they were eating, they were drinking . . . but on the day that Lot went out from Sodom it rained fire and brimstone from heaven and destroyed them all. (Lk. 17:24, 28–29)

> It is only just for God to repay with affliction those who afflict you, and to give relief to you who are afflicted and to us as well

when the Lord Jesus shall be revealed from heaven with His
mighty angels in flaming fire, dealing out retribution to those
who do not know God and those who do not obey the gospel
of our Lord Jesus. (2 Thes. 1:7)

While these passages employ a variety of images and similes
to express the coming judgment, they are all prophecies of a
Sodom-like judgment on Israel. John is speaking directly to the
Pharisees when he warns them about the axe at the root and alludes to Isaiah's prophecy about Assyria (Is. 10:15–19) to warn
that another Assyria is going to cut down the forest of Israel.
Jesus' parable of the tares has been interpreted for centuries as a
parable about the church age, but it makes much better sense as a
parabolic description of the post-exilic history of Israel. With the
return from exile, Yahweh sowed the land with the seed of man
and beast, but since that time Satan has been busy sowing tares
among the wheat. Jesus has now come with His winnowing fork,
and before the end of the age, the wheat and tares will be separated. The end of the age thus refers not to the final judgment but
to the close of "this generation." As we have noted in a previous
chapter, the example of Lot is used to describe the coming judgment on the wicked city of Jerusodom, and Paul's assurance that
Jesus will come with angels "in flaming fire" is assurance only if it
refers to relief for the afflicted Thessalonians. These are the
prophecies to which Peter refers: by the word of Jesus and the
"beloved brother" Paul, the "now" heavens and earth have been
reserved for fire.

I have already mentioned the parallel between the sequence in
chapters 2 and 3, Flood/Sodom is water/fire; water from heaven,
fire from heaven.[13] Peter describes the earlier judgment of the
world and the coming judgment in terms of the two archetypal

---

[13] Bauckham, *Jude, 2 Peter,* 252.

divine judgments in Genesis. The destruction of the present heavens and earth is parallel in a sense to the flood, but in some ways more specifically parallel to the destruction of the cities of the plain. This fits with the descriptions of Jerusalem as Sodom in Revelation as well as Jesus' warnings about Sodom in the Gospels.

Peter divides history into three large periods:

1. From creation by water to destruction by water.
2. From formation of the "now" heavens and earth to "the day of God."
3. The "new heavens and new earth in which righteousness dwells" that follows the day of God.

The history of Israel is absorbed into a larger scheme here, and what is destined for fire is the world that has existed since the flood, not merely the Mosaic world.

Peter expands on the prophecy of the coming destruction in verses 10–13. What is he referring to? Does the phrase "heaven and earth" refer to the physical universe, or is it a description of an historical order? As noted earlier in this commentary, the phrase can have both connotations. Which is more likely in 2 Peter 3? My arguments throughout this commentary set the context for answering these questions, and I believe establish that Peter is talking about the destruction of the Old Creation. An examination of the passage itself supports this.

For starters, we can make some observations about what is actually said here. According to verse 7, the present heavens and earth are reserved for fire, which implies that both heaven and earth are being kept for the day of judgment. In verses 10–13, however, a distinction is made, like the distinction in the mode of creation (heaven by word, earth by water): heaven passes away, while the earth is "discovered" (*eurethesetai*). In verses 10 and 12 the elements (*stoicheia*) are associated with the heavens, in that both are burned, "pass away," are "destroyed," or "melt." Whatever the *stoicheia* are, they are associated here with the heavens. Two key conclusions follow from these observations:

1. Peter is not describing a cosmic conflagration. If this passage is taken as the literal destruction of the universe, it is only the heavens that are being destroyed, or rather, the heavens and their elements.

2. This, further, makes it virtually impossible that Peter is describing the physical universe at all. Can we imagine a situation in which the physical heavens (outer space with all its planets) melt in intense heat but do not destroy the earth? Would it make any sense to say that after the heavens are burned to ash and molten elements, the earth is "discovered"? I am no scientist, but I should think "discovered" is the last thing the earth would be under those circumstances.

The progression of Peter's terminology also needs to be carefully examined. According to verses 5–7, (1) The "heavens and earth" existed long ago; (2) by the word and water, the *kosmos* of that time, the *kosmos* of the pre-flood world, was destroyed; (3) but the "now" heavens and earth are being reserved for fire.

"Heavens and earth" in verse 7 appears to be used in a different sense from verse 5, which describes the regions of the original physical creation.[14] The "present heavens and earth," precisely because they are called the *present* heavens and earth, cannot be the same as the *created* heavens and earth. That would make "present" redundant. Verse 6 thus says that the flood is a watershed between two different "worlds," two different "heavens and earth." The old world was destroyed in the flood, and the world that came into being after the flood is the "present heavens and earth."

Physically, however, the "present heavens and earth" are the same as the "heavens and earth" of creation: we still have sky, earth,

---

[14] Against Moo, who recognizes that "world" in verse 6 does not mean "the physical universe," but argues that verse 7, by returning to the phrase "heaven and earth," does refer to the physical universe (*2 Peter, Jude,* 171).

and sea, birds, animals and fish, fruit-bearing trees and grasses of the field. Peter, however, distinguishes the "heavens and earth" of creation from the "now" heavens and earth. Verse 7 thus cannot refer to the physical heavens and earth.[15] Thus there are contextual grounds within 2 Peter 3 (not to mention the rest of 2 Peter) for saying that the phrase "heaven and earth" refers to a political world-order rather than to the physical universe. The destruction of the heavens and the discovery of the earth refer not to the end of the cosmos but to the end of the Old Creation order. It is used to describe the end of a religious and political order, as it often is in prophecy (Is. 13:13; 34:4; 51:15–16; 65:17; Jer. 4:23–31; Heb. 12:26).

Every commentator on 2 Peter I have read has struggled to make sense of the earth being "found" or "discovered." Difficult as this is, I believe it is a key to a full understanding of the whole passage and that it can be best understood when we recognize that Peter is describing the end of the Old Creation. Most interpreters recognize that the idea is judicial: the effect of the day of judgment on the earth is to expose the ungodly and bring them into judgment. Heaven and the *stoicheia* are thus a kind of barrier between God and the earth and its works so that the removal of heaven leaves the earth exposed.[16] The wicked will be "found" out in their wickedness, despite their apparent efforts to hide themselves from the wrath of the Lamb:

[15] *Kosmos* in verse 6 has, moreover, a specific reference to the cosmos of the ungodly, which is evident from comparison with 2:5. The "world of the ungodly" was destroyed in the flood, and this is also mentioned in 3:7. The fiery destruction of the present heavens and earth parallels the flood, and this fiery judgment is going to be for the "destruction of ungodly men."

[16] This makes a neat contrast with verse 14, where Peter exhorts his readers to be "found by Him in peace." Peter's readers are to be diligent so that they do not stand naked and ashamed in the judgment, but spotless and blameless, fitting sacrifices to God.

And the kings of the earth and the great men and the com-
manders and the rich and the strong and every slave and free
man [seven categories] hid themselves in the caves and among
the rocks of the mountains; and they said to the mountains and
to the rocks, "Fall on us and hide us from the face of Him who
sits on the throne, and from the wrath of the Lamb; for the
great day of their wrath has come; and who is able to stand?"
(Rev. 6:15–17)

To unravel this further, I suggest that "heavens" here refers specifically to the firmament heavens, and therefore the removal of
the "firmament" leads to the "discovery" of the earth. Four observations support this:

1. Peter says that the heavens came into being by the "word" of the
Lord, and this applies strictly to the firmament heavens. Genesis
1:1 refers to the highest heavens, the dwelling of God, but it does
not say that the heavens were created by the word. Though it is
likely that the highest heavens *were* formed by the word, Genesis 1
says only that the firmament-heavens were created by the word
(vv. 6–8). Thus 2 Peter 2:5 is talking about the firmament, not the
highest heavens.

2. "Elements" (*stoicheia*) are placed in the heavens. Commentators point out that *stoicheia* is sometimes used of heavenly bodies,
whether stars or heavenly beings like angels. If the word refers to
heavenly bodies, then the heavens in which they are placed must be
the firmament (Gen. 1:14–19).

3. That the word for "heavens" is plural is not relevant. Genesis
1:8 says that the firmament is called "heaven," but as always in the
Old Testament, the Hebrew word is *shemayim*, a dual form that can
be translated as a plural. Peter is adopting Semitic terminology
here and referring to the firmament with the plural form.

4. Considering the firmament helps to explain how the "heavens and earth" of the postdiluvian period are a different world from
the prediluvian heavens and earth. After the flood, Noah offered

sacrifices to the Lord, and the Lord smelled a soothing aroma. The sacrificial smoke ascended through the firmament to the nostrils of God. Yahweh then set a bow in the firmament and promised to remember His covenant when He looks at it. Something new entered the firmament after the flood, just as there were changes in the arrangement of things on earth. Noah was the New Adam in a new heavens and earth.

What Peter describes is thus an end to the world of the Noahic order. After the Parousia of Jesus, the Noahic order will no longer exist. No longer will sacrifice be offered, as it has been since Noah. When Yahweh called Abram, He drew a distinction within humanity between Jew and Gentile, but this distinction was set in the larger background of the Noahic covenant. In A.D. 70, this arrangement came to an end.

But doesn't the rainbow still appear in the firmament? And what does this have to do with the destruction of the Jerusalem temple in A.D. 70? These questions can be answered by recognizing that the Noahic order took a more specific form with the call of Abram, the establishment of Israel and Torah, and the building of the tabernacle. James Jordan has argued that the tabernacle is an architectural form of the cloud of God's glory, complete with smoke ascending as a soothing aroma to God and a rainbow around God's throne.[17] The colorful tabernacle curtains form a rainbow environment, and the tabernacle as a whole was an architectural form of the firmament, the antechamber of heaven, through which man passes to reach God. In the tabernacle and temple, the firmament comes to earth.

In this context, the *stoicheia* are lights and other vessels in the temple, the articles of temple service. For Peter, *stoicheia* has a

---

[17] See Jordan's extensive series of lectures on the tabernacle in his taped lectures on Exodus, available from Biblical Horizons, P.O. Box 1096, Niceville, FL 32588.

very full connotation, alluding to the idea of heavenly powers, perhaps to angels, and to the "elementary principles" of the Old Covenant order. The latter meaning is especially prominent, for
elsewhere in the New Testament, this word always refers to the
practices and institutions of the Old Covenant order, whether they
are the practices of the Jewish law or the parallel practices of Gentile paganism:

> So also we [Jews], while we were children, were held in bond-
> age under the elementary things [*stoicheia*] of the world. . . . But
> now that you [Gentiles] have come to know God, or rather to
> be known by God, how is it that you turn back again to the
> weak and worthless elementary things [*stoicheia*], to which you
> desire to be enslaved all over again? (Gal. 4:3, 9)

> See to it that no one takes you captive through philosophy and
> empty deception, according to the tradition of men, according
> to the elementary things [*stoicheia*] of the world, rather than ac-
> cording to Christ. . . . If you have died with Christ to the el-
> ementary things [*stoicheia*] of the world, why, as if living in the
> world, do you submit yourselves to decrees, such as "Do not
> handle, do not taste, do not touch." (Col. 2:8, 20–21)

> For though by this time you ought to be teachers, you have
> need again for someone to teach you the elementary things
> [*stoicheia*] of the oracles of God, and you have come to need
> milk and not solid food. (Heb. 5:12)

So long as the "firmament" of the temple has standing, and sacrifices are being offered, God remains in His rainbow environment
and looks favorably on the people. But with the destruction of the
temple, the "firmament" and its *stoicheia* are burned up, and the
earth (land) and its inhabitants are exposed to God's full view. The
veil that separates the fiery wrath of God from sinful Israel is
burned away, and the earth and its works are "found out." God will

no longer look at the works of the earth through the rainbow, through the firmament of the temple. And that means that there will be no way of atonement, no way of access to God, other than through the true firmament-mediator, the God-Man Jesus Christ. This destruction of the temple-firmament and the exposure of the earth is a judgment that is followed by the establishment of a new "firmament" and a new earth. The new heavens are the church. God dwells among us, and in Christ we are the rainbow through which God views the world. [18] With the removal of the firmament temple and following the purging of the earth by fire, the new heavens and earth comes fully into reality. [19]

A THOUSAND YEARS

Verse 9 has been seen as undermining the sense of imminence we find elsewhere in the letter and in the rest of the New Testament. With his reference to the "time" of God, Peter is said to "transcend" the scrupulous (and rather lowbrow) concern about timetables. In

[18] Perhaps this means that the rainbow, though it still appears in the firmament, no longer has the covenantal importance it had prior to the end of the Old Creation. Now, Christ Jesus and His church surround the throne of God and form the multicolored lens set in the heavens.

[19] Compare the related interpretation of W. E. Wilson, as summarized by Bauckham: "[W]hen the intervening heavens are burned away, the earth and its works, from the divine point of view, become visible. This provides an ironic contrast with the picture of the wicked trying to hide from God at his eschatological coming to judgment (Is. 2:19; Hos. 10:8; Rev. 6:15–18). Thus the author 'with a fine sense of climax makes the passing away of the heavens and the destruction of the intermediate spiritual beings, while terrible in themselves, even more terrible in that they lead up to the discovery, naked and unprotected on the earth, of men and all their works by God. This Judgment is here represented not so much as a destructive act of God, as a revelation of him from which none can escape'" (Bauckham, *Jude, 2 Peter,* 319; the original article was in *Expository Times* [1920–1921], 44–45). Wilson, of course, is still seeing the "heavens" as the "physical" firmament and does not connect this with the destruction of the temple, though his comments are very suggestive.

essence, this line of argument is gnostic. God is a God of timetables, the God who revealed a calendar to Israel with very specific dates, who promised to redeem Israel from Egypt four hundred years after Abraham, who brought Israel out in the fourth generation, who delivered the Jews from Babylonian captivity after seventy years, and who then promised to send Messiah after an additional "seventy weeks of years." Scripture, and the God revealed in Scripture, is concerned with specific times and seasons. When He says He will do something within a period of time, He will do it. That is what it means to be God.

Apart from these global theological issues, it is highly unlikely that Peter would respond to the mockers by dodging (or "transcending") the question of timing. As we have seen, the whole dispute about the Parousia is about its timing: Jesus promised to come before the apostolic generation had passed, but now the fathers are falling asleep and Jesus is nowhere to be found. If Peter suddenly offered an argument that avoided the question of timing, he would be playing into the mockers' hands. They would respond with even deeper skepticism, since they would conclude that, as far as the apostle Peter is concerned, statements about time are not statements about time. We can be fairly confident that, if the letter is coherent at all, Peter is not doing this.

Instead, Peter is responding to the delay of the Parousia with two arguments. The first is from Psalm 90:4. The Psalm of Moses is a meditation on the contrast between God's eternity and the brevity of human life. What is a long time for man is only yesterday for God. He has all the time He needs; He is not so much timeless but, as Robert Jenson puts it, time-ful. How does this respond to the mockers? Peter is not emptying temporal statements of meaning; he is not saying that Jesus might be interpreted as saying that the Parousia would not happen for millennia. Nor is he saying that "this generation" might actually mean "the rest of world history" or that "some of you standing here will not taste death" might actually mean "all of you standing here will taste death." Rather, Peter is saying simply that what appears to be a lengthy delay to us is nothing to God. Peter is making no comment here about the timing of the Parousia, for he wrote the entire letter to insist that the timing will be just as Jesus promised.

This goes hand in hand with the second response, in verse 9. The Parousia is "delayed" because God is being patient. In 1 Peter, Peter has already referred to the patience of God in the time leading up to the flood. God gave Noah time to build an ark and He gave the wicked time to repent or harden themselves. God's "delay," which is not a delay at all, is an opportunity for repentance and also fills up the fullness of the sins of Canaan. The Lord is patient toward "you," the believers to whom Peter is writing. He is patient toward them so that they can get their act together, so that none perish but all come to repentance. False teachers, and those whom they have led astray, should not harden themselves; judgment will come, but God is giving them time to turn around. Far from supporting the mockers' skepticism, the apparent delay is designed to give them a chance to renounce their skepticism.

Revelation gives us an additional reason for the delay of the powerful coming of Jesus. As the fifth seal is opened at the beginning of the book, the souls under the altar are revealed and are crying out for God to avenge their blood that has been shed in martyrdom (Rev. 6:9–10). They are not given immediate satisfaction:

> And there was given to each of them a white robe; and they were told that they should rest for a little while longer, until the number of their fellow servants and their brethren who were to be killed, even as they had been, should be completed also. (6:11)

During the sixth seal, we see these additional brethren and servants, 144,000 Jewish believers, sealed for their protection (7:1–8). Once they are killed and join the souls under the altar, then the end will come. And this is what happens in Revelation 14: the

144,000 are the "firstfruits to God and to the Lamb" (14:4), and by
the end of the chapter these firstfruits of grain and grapes have been
harvested by the Son of Man riding on a cloud (14:14–20). Their
blood is squeezed out and poured by the bowl-angels onto the harlot city, and this brings the end of the city (chaps. 16–18). In short,
the delay of the final end, the delay of Jesus' coming in judgment
against the harlot, occurs because the number of Jewish believers
and martyrs needs to be filled up. The delay that Peter talks about is
for the same reason: Peter, writing to Jewish believers, says that
the Lord is giving time for all the remnant of Israel to be gathered
and harvested into the kingdom. So all Israel will be saved, and
when that occurs, the end will come.

SCRIPTURE INDEX

8:22 92
26:11 64, 86

Isaiah
1:7–10 56
2:19 102
3:8–9a 56
10:15–19 95
13:13 98
13:19 57
28:1–2 57
34:4 98
42:1 24
42:8 27
42:12 27
48:20 24
51:15–16 98
63:7 27
65 3
65:17 98

Jeremiah
2:5 16
4:23–31 98
6:13 51
10:2–3 16
10:14–15 16
17:15 85
23:14 56
26 51
27:9 51
28:1 51
28:13 51
28:17 52
39:34 63
49:18 57
50:40 57

Lamentations
4:6 56

Ezekiel
16 60, 75
16:15 60
16:25 60
16:28 60
16:46 57
16:48–49 57
16:49 73
16:55–56 57
23 75
37 5

Daniel
2:28 81
2:38 81
7 44, 82
9 81
9:26 57
10:14 81
11 81

Hosea
1:10 15
2:23 15
10:8 102

Joel
2:17 85

Nahum
1:8 57

Habakkuk
3:3 27

Zechariah
13:2 51

Malachi
2:17 85

Matthew
3:7 41
3:8–12 94
10:1–2 24
11:16 41
12:34 41
12:39 41
12:41–42 41
12:43–45 62
12:45 41, 62
13:40–42 94
16 41
16:4 41
16:27 41
16:28 2, 40, 41
17:1 43
17:17 41
21:34 24
23:33 41
23:34–36 72
23:36 41
24 3, 41
24:1–35 41
24:3 41
24:4–8 48
24:9–14 48
24:11 48
24:22–25 48
24:30–31 41
24:34 41
24:37 55
24:48–50 48
24:51 48

Mark
9:1 40, 43
9:2 40
13 3

CPSIA information can be obtained
at www.ICGtesting.com
Printed in the USA
FSOW01n0948020115
4303FS